At last after fourteen years of bein
this is the only set of profession
that successfully translates and a
language and culture of our dep
he writes like one of us and this sho....
a way that hits the heart and mind whilst giving a realistic picture of the joy
and struggles faced by council estate Christians.

> **Ian Williamson** is the pastor of New Life Church, Middlesbrough,
> England, and has been involved in full time Christian ministry since
> 2007. Ian has served as a chaplain in the local prisons prior to
> planting a church in a disadvantaged community.

If you want a book about the real and daily struggles of following Christ
which pulls no punches, dodges no controversy, fudges no issue and gives
it to you straight, then here it is. *War* is a great book to give to young
Christians. It is also an excellent example of how to teach vital truth in an
accessible way. I don't know anyone who wouldn't benefit from reading
it. I certainly did.

> **Steve Timmis** has many years of experience with churches both
> large and small. He is Global Director of Acts 29 and pastor at
> The Crowded House in Sheffield, England.

Too many believe that Jesus is supposed to take away all of their problems.
This book will help me explain to them that the spiritual life is war. Mez
keeps it real and speak truth. I love these guys.

> **Joel Kurtz** leads The Garden, a church in the heart of one of
> Baltimore's most deprived communities.

To say that I'm grateful for Mez's ministry and work (especially on this project)
would be an understatement. Over the years, I've come to appreciate Mez
not just as excellent philosopher and pastor, but as a practitioner. The way
that he simply tackles complex truths and make it accessible to an audience
that is in desperate need of resources like this is a labor of love that becomes
apparent from the first pages. I'm excited about the role this book will play
in discipling the very people this book was written for.

> **John Onwuchekwa** is Lead Pastor at Cornerstone Church, Atlanta

WAR

WHY DID LIFE JUST GET HARDER?

MEZ MCCONNELL

CHRISTIAN
FOCUS

Copyright © Mez McConnell 2017

paperback ISBN 978-1-78191-711-4
epub ISBN 978-1-78191-925-5
mobi ISBN 978-1-78191-926-2

10 9 8 7 6 5 4 3 2 1

Published in 2017
by
Christian Focus Publications Ltd,
Geanies House, Fearn, Ross-shire,
IV20 1TW, Great Britain.

www.christianfocus.com

Cover and Interior Design:
Moose77.com

Printed and bound
by
Bell & Bain, Glasgow

CONTENTS

PREFACE

I didn't grow up going to church. Christianity was something completely alien to me. I grew up on the street and the only time I went to a church was to bury a friend who died too young. God, in his grace, saved me after I got out of prison. When I first went to church it seemed such a strange place. Now I am a pastor in a poor community called Niddrie in Edinburgh. There are so few helpful books and resources that are relatable to people in my community. That is why we wrote this series of books. Accessible, relatable and interactive workbooks for new Christians living in unchurched and disadvantaged communities. For this book I asked Brian Davis to help me. He is a pastor at the Risen Christ Fellowship in inner city Philadelphia. I pray that as you study this book you will grow stronger in your faith

Mez McConnell
Pastor Niddrie Communty Church
Director 20schemes

INTRODUCTION

The First Steps to Discipleship series will help equip those from an un-churched background take the first steps in following Jesus. We call this the 'pathway to service' as we believe that every Christian should be equipped to be of service to Christ and His church no matter your background or life experience.

If you are a church leader doing ministry in hard places use these books as a tool to help grow those who are unfamiliar with the teachings of Jesus into new disciples. These books will equip them to grow in character, knowledge and action.

Or if you yourself are new to the Christian faith, still struggling to make sense of what a Christian is, or what the Bible actually says, then this is an easy to understand guide as you take your first steps as a follower of Jesus.

There are many ways to use these books.

• They could be used by an individual who simply reads through the content and works through the questions on their own.
• They could be used in a one-to-one setting, where two people read through the material before they meet and then discuss the questions together.
• They could be used in a group setting where a leader presents the material as a talk, stopping for group discussion throughout.

Your setting will determine how you best use this resource.

A User's Key:
As you work through the studies you will come across the following symbols...

 Joe's Story — At the start of each chapter you'll meet Joe and hear something about his story and what's been going on in his life. We want you to take what we've been learning from the Bible and work out what difference it would make in Joe's life. So whenever you see this symbol you'll hear some more about Joe's story.

 Illustration — Through real life examples and scenarios, these sections help us to understand the point that's being made.

STOP — When we hit an important or hard point we'll ask you to stop and spend some time thinking or chatting through what we've just learnt. This might be answering some questions, or it might be hearing more of Joe's story.

 Read 3x — The Bible is God's word to us, and therefore it is the final word to us on everything we are to believe and how we are to behave. Therefore we want to read the Bible first, and we want to read it carefully. So whenever you see this symbol you are to read or listen to the Bible passage three times. If the person you're reading the Bible with feels comfortable, get them to read it at least once.

 Memory Verse — At the end of each chapter we'll suggest a Bible verse for memorisation. We have found Bible memorisation to be really effective in our context. The verse (or verses) will be directly related to what we've covered in the chapter.

 Summary — Also, at the end of each chapter we've included a short summary of the content of that chapter. If you're working your way through the book with another person, this might be useful to revisit when picking up from a previous week.

MEET JOE

The early years

Joe has never ventured far from where he was born in downtown Baltimore. He doesn't know his dad who ended up in prison when he was a baby and died before Joe was eighteen. His Mom is an alcoholic and gambling addict. They haven't spoken much since he moved in his with Gran when he was a young boy at elementary school. Growing up in poverty in the inner city meant that Joe had to grow up fast. He didn't do well at school, not because he isn't capable but because he never tried. He served two separate jail terms for stealing cars in his twenties.

Life Now

Now in his late forties, Joe has lived a life of petty crime, never holding down a real job for very long, drinking too much, and hooked on heroin. He loves playing Basketball with the guys in the park and he is popular and well known in the community. He has three kids and lives with the mother of his youngest daughter. He is in an on and off again relationship with his wife. Joe has slept around but always comes back home to her. His two sons have left home and have their own run in's with the law and trouble with drugs. His daughter is sixteen and lives with Joe and her mother. Joe will do anything for her.

Joe's Gran took him to church as a kid but it was never a big part of his life. He went to church camps and he always felt good in church but didn't see it as a place where he belonged. He had only really gone to church for the funerals of his good friends who died young.

It was at one of those funerals that Joe began to really think hard about life and death. The Preacher seemed to be shouting at him from the pulpit telling him that if he does not repent then he would go to Hell, but Jesus, the Son of God, has come to take away his sins if he would turn to him. At the time it made no sense at all, but Joe became unsettled about death, Hell and Jesus. He couldn't stop thinking about it. Not long after, he and his wife went to church with his Gran and that is where Joe hears the Gospel, believes in Jesus, and repents of his sin. He becomes a Christian but no one prepared him for just how hard things were about to become.

This is Joe's story…

WHAT'S THE POINT?

WHEN WE ARE SAVED BY JESUS WE ENTER A LIFELONG SPIRITUAL WAR.

WELCOME TO THE WAR!

JOE'S STORY

It's been a couple of months since Joe made a profession of faith in Jesus. Initially, he was really excited about his new found faith. He felt like the weight of the world had been lifted off his shoulders. He told everybody he could think of: his family, his neighbours, his friends and even associates from his drug dealing days. The response was mixed. Some people were happy for him. Others were confused by what he was saying. A few people laughed at him and told him he'd grow out of it. Very few opposed him publicly but, recently, he has discovered that some people, including family members, were mocking him on social media.

He is very upset and angry. He's not used to people treating him like this. People used to have respect for him. They used to fear him. He doesn't know how to act. He doesn't know what's going on. He feels so confused. One minute he is on top of the world and the next he is really depressed. One minute he is sure of God and the next he is full of doubts. Why are his friends and family being so dismissive of his new found faith? Why can't they be happy that he is trying to get his life in order? What's happening to him?

STOP

Q: What do you think is going on in Joe's life? Why do you think the people around him are acting like this?

ILLUSTRATION

During the first Gulf War in 1990, retreating Iraqi forces engaged in a 'scorched earth' policy of setting fire to as many Kuwaiti oil wells as they could. They had lost the war but still wanted to cause as much damage they could to hamper the progress of the coalition forces as they moved back in. Their aim was merely to frustrate the advancing army in a final act of desperation.

This is exactly what is going on in Joe's life right now. Colossians 2:14-15 teaches us that when Jesus went to the cross, 'He disarmed the rulers and authorities and put them to open shame, by triumphing over them in him.' In other words, Jesus has fully and finally defeated the devil. All that the devil is doing now is engaging in his own scorched earth policy with his army of demons. Joe is now experiencing first hand the reality of the spiritual battle that every person becomes involved in once they hand their lives over to Jesus Christ.

This is part of what it means to 'count the cost' of being a Christian.

Joe needs to learn that now, and for the rest of his life, he is in an all out, no holds barred, spiritual war.

Some people think that Christianity is a way to an easier, happier life. They assume that since someone is right with God that all will be fine with their world.

Of course, it is true that when people, by faith, repent of their sins and look to Jesus for forgiveness, life does get better. At least, spiritually speaking.

It is true that
eternal life is far better than eternal death.

It is true that

heaven is better than hell.

It is false that

life gets easier when we become a Christian.

It is true that

when people come to Jesus for new life they are at the same time leaving their old life behind.

It is true that

they have *'switched sides'* on the spiritual battle going on for the souls of men, women and children around the globe.

It is true that

King Jesus is far superior to the ruler they used to have in their life.

It is false that

this old ruler is going to go down without a fight.

It is true that

the devil is very angry and hostile to Jesus and is the sworn enemy of every Christian.

 ## ILLUSTRATION

There used to be a children's game called *'King of the Hill'*. After locating a fairly climbable hill or pile of dirt, someone would climb to the top of the hill and be declared the *'King of the Hill'*. The easy part was climbing up the hill quickly. The difficult part was staying on top as the designated *'King'*. All the other players would constantly climb the hill and try to throw, pull and push the present *'King'* off the top of the hill so that they themselves could be crowned the *'King'* in their place. Depending on who was playing, the game could get quite rough fairly quickly!

In a similar way, now that we have crowned Jesus as the King of our lives,
all the enemies of God are violently opposed to us.

Not only do they
seek to tear us away from Jesus.

But they
want one of His enemies to reign over us in His place.

From the first moment we are saved in Christ, war has been declared against us by those who want us to give up on Christ and go back to our old way of living.

Unlike a game that comes to an end within hours, they will try and oppose our commitment to Jesus until the day we die.

Now Joe, much like the rest of the world, had no idea that after coming to Jesus he would have to battle the devil and a load of demons! That seems a little bit weird and also terrifying at the same time. But, it is important for Joe to know the full story of the spiritual battle that he has now signed up for.

For our struggle is not against flesh and blood, but against the rulers, against the authorities, against the powers of this dark world and against the spiritual forces of evil in the heavenly realms. **Ephesians 6:12** (NIV)

STOP

Q: Why is it so important for Joe to understand that he is now involved in a spiritual battle?

These truths will help Joe to see that what he is experiencing is not new. It is not unique to him. Every single Christian in history has been through it. <u>Every single Christian in the world is battling the enemy every single day of their lives</u>. Joe needs to understand that this swirl of emotions he is caught in is a perfectly natural reaction to what is going on in his life.

In fact, Joe is fighting a coalition of evil. There is 'Satan', his old ruler, and his tag-team partners in crime, 'the flesh' and 'the world'. Together, these forces of darkness are seeking to kill Joe's faith.

These three have one job and one job only.

They are thieves seeking to steal away Joe's newfound joy in Jesus.

> ## JOE
> *But why is this happening to me now? Why didn't the devil attack me when I was doing heroin or breaking into cars? Where was he then?*

The problem for Joe, as it is for all unbelievers, is that before Jesus saved him he was dead in his sins. That means he had no clue that he was under the control of the devil and the dark forces of evil. This is how the Apostle Paul puts it in **Ephesians 2:1-3** (NIV):

'And you were dead in the trespasses and sins in which you once walked, following the course of this world, following the prince of the power of the air, the spirit that is now at work in the sons of disobedience – among whom we all once lived in the passions of our flesh, carrying out the desires of the body and the mind, and were by nature children of wrath, like the rest of mankind.'

Joe needs to know several things about himself and the devil from these verses.

Firstly, before coming to faith in Christ, we clearly see that <u>we were dead in our trespasses and sins</u>. We weren't merely in bad shape, but dead shape. Not only were we spiritually dead, we were <u>'following the course of this world'</u>. (We are going to find out more about this phrase in chapter 2.)

Secondly , <u>we see that this 'world' has a ruler</u>. In fact, before Jesus saved us we all followed the <u>prince of the power of the air</u>. He is also known as <u>'the spirit now at work in the sons of disobedience'</u>.

This prince, we are told, is leading the world, and all those in it, in complete disobedience to God.

Now who is this *'prince'* leading people to do evil? Who is this father of the sons of disobedience? It is the devil himself.

JOE

Hang on, says Joe. I thought the Bible taught that we are all God's children. Are you saying my friends and family are all children of the devil? Do they belong to the Devil?

Yes! That is exactly what the Bible is teaching. Many people wrongly say that we are all God's children but this is <u>never something Jesus communicates</u>. He actually says the complete opposite! When Jesus was responding to people who refused to obey His word, who rejected His teaching, He plainly tells them that they are not the children of God and explains why they do not believe Him. *'For you are the children of your father the devil, and you love to do the evil things he does.'* (John 8:44 NLT) <u>Jesus always tells it like it is</u>. (We are going to look at the devil in more detail in chapter 4.)

Thirdly, not only are we dead in our sins and under the influence of the world, and the devil, <u>we love to disobey God</u>. It's what we naturally long to do. <u>We desire to be disobedient!</u> That's what Paul means when he tells us that before Jesus saved us, *'We all once lived in the <u>passions of our flesh</u>, carrying out the desires of the body and the mind'*. (We are going to look at this in more detail in chapter 3.) The point is simply this:

We can't claim that the world and the devil make us sin because it's something we deeply desire to do on our own as well.

JOE

This all sounds a bit hardcore. What's the point of trying to be a Christian if I've got to go through this for the rest of my life? I might as well give up now, right?

The short answer to Joe's question is no! We could be tempted into thinking that it would be better to go back to our old way of life instead of face the trials and temptations of living for Jesus. But God has got plans for all of His people <u>and those plans are, ultimately, good for us</u>.

'And we know that for those who love God all things work together for good, for those who are called according to His purpose.' **Romans 8:28**

Even in the midst of our spiritual battles, God is working for our good. If God has given us a way to be forgiven in Jesus, don't you think He would give us a way to be victorious in our warfare through Jesus? Of course He does! While we war, we do not go to battle unsure of our victory. We are to be entirely confident and assured that we will be victorious in our warfare. The same faith that was needed to initially trust God for salvation, will be continually needed to stand strong in our relationship with the Lord – even in the face of opposition. Here are merely three (of many!) reasons we can have such confidence.

We are well protected. Jesus secured our protection in His prayer for us to His Father, 'I do not ask that you take them out of the world, but that you keep them from the evil one.' (John 17:15) Jesus has pledged God's protection to us through His prayers for us. This is more than just protection from the devil, but also protection from our sin. He has prayed for us so that our faith would not fail. This is why in the Bible Christians are referred to as, *'...those who are called, beloved in God the Father and kept for Jesus Christ.'* (Jude 1)

We are well empowered. When thinking about the spiritual battles we are facing we may be tempted to despair. They seem to be massively strong influences and Joe is concerned if he will be strong enough to fight them. It's one thing to think about a fist fight, one on one, man-to-man. But this? How can he even begin to fight a spiritual battle against such strong enemies? Well Joe is right to question, but wrong to be concerned. The Bible tells us something amazing about God's power working in us. Like a grown man doesn't need to fear the strength of a toddler, so a Christian doesn't need to fear the strength of our enemies... because God has given us His strength through His spirit! *'...for He who is in you is greater than He who is in the world'*. (1 John 4:4)

We are well equipped. God has not left us to fend for ourselves in coming up with a battle plan. Just as it is with our salvation, God has richly provided us with everything we need for life and godliness. This means that everything we need to be godly and growing in our relationship with God has been given to us, including what we need to be found victorious in our spiritual war. For instance, we are told that God has given weapons with which to wage war. He didn't give us rocket launchers with our Bibles, or physical swords when we finally understood the gospel. We don't have flesh-and-blood enemies for the most part, but spiritual enemies. So understandably, the weapons He gave us are spiritual. *'For though we walk in the flesh, we are not waging war according to the flesh. For the weapons of our warfare are not of the flesh but have divine power to destroy strongholds.'* (2 Cor. 10:3-4)

There are many ways that God protects, empowers and equips us to be victorious in our lifelong war against sin. He has secured our victory over the three-headed enemy called *'the world, the flesh and the devil'*. There is always a war for our souls, and we must always be involved in the fight. The mere act of God giving us weapons should communicate strongly to us that we should be fighting with them. But Joe doesn't know where to begin.

<u>So he should begin where all warriors begin — dressing themselves for battle.</u>

ILLUSTRATION

Imagine going to a funeral dressed in shorts and flip flops. What about turning up to a job interview in ripped jeans and a stained tee-shirt? What if the President or Prime Minister turned up to a cabinet meeting in his pyjamas? Would that be appropriate? Probably not. How we dress should reflect the situation we find ourselves in or the occasion we are attending. We all know that there is a dress code for different situations. We wouldn't dream of going out to war in a pair of swimming trunks! No self respecting soldier would go out to battle without remembering to put on his body armour. Wearing the wrong outfit to a formal party could be embarrassing at most, whereas wearing the wrong, or no, armour in war could be fatal.

The Bible has clear instructions on how Christians ought to clothe themselves for the battle of their lives. In fact, it is the book of Ephesians, yet again, that points us to some of the soberest and most helpful instruction about arming ourselves for spiritual warfare.

'Finally, be strong in the Lord and in the strength of his might. Put on the whole armour of God, that you may be able to stand against the _schemes of the devil_. For we do not _wrestle against_ flesh and blood, but against the rulers, against the authorities, against the cosmic powers over this present darkness, against the spiritual forces of evil in the heavenly places. Therefore, _take up the whole armour of God_, that you may _be able to withstand_ in the evil day, and having done all, to stand firm.' **Ephesians 6:10-13**

Here we are told to ready ourselves for battle and clothe ourselves with appropriate attire. He doesn't call us to go grab the bulletproof vests or hazmat suits. We are called to be clothed in the whole armour of God. But Ephesians 6 doesn't stop there. It continues in verses 14-17:

Stand firm then, with the belt of truth buckled around your waist, with the breastplate of righteousness in place, and with your feet fitted with the readiness that comes from the gospel of peace. In addition to all this, take up the shield of faith, with which you can extinguish all the flaming arrows of the evil one. Take the helmet of salvation and the sword of the Spirit, which is the word of God. (NIV)

Notice, the language used in these verses.

Belt of truth.
    Breastplate of righteousness.
Shield of faith.
    The helmet of salvation.
The sword of the Spirit.

Even our shoes should be tightly tied with the 'gospel of peace' as we prepare ourselves for action. Without this clothing we will not be able to extinguish the flaming darts of the evil one. Unless we dress for war then we will fail to keep alert and we will fail to stand in the face of the onslaught from the evil one.

MEMORY VERSE

'Put on the whole armour of God, that you may be able to stand against the schemes of the devil.' (Eph. 6:11)

 SUMMARY

Joe needs to know that when he signed up to follow Jesus, he signed up to fight a war. This is not a short war, but rather a war for life. However, God hasn't left Joe, or any of His people, to fight alone. He has given us all we need to fight and end up victorious.

But before any of us can fight the war well, we had better understand our enemies and their plans a little better...

WHAT'S THE POINT?

THE WHOLE WORLD IS HOSTILE TO THE THINGS OF GOD.

ENEMY 1:
THE WORLD

JOE

Joe is confused. He's trying to live a Christian life. He's trying to be a better husband and a better dad. He's removed all of the drug paraphernalia from the house and informed all the local dealers that he's stopped selling and taking. But people just seem to be trying to trip him up all the time. People are offering him free drugs. Guys who used to be scared of him are getting in his face. He feels like they're disrespecting him. Women are chatting him up and it just seems that everywhere he turns people are waiting for him to make a mistake. He understands that he's in a spiritual battle but that doesn't make it any easier.

Let's go back to the book of Ephesians 2:2 where we came across the phrase, 'the world'. Let's look at a key passage in the Bible as we try and understand what we mean by battling against the world.

'Do not love the world or anything in the world. If anyone loves the world, the love of the Father is not in him. For everything in the world – the cravings of sinful man, the lust of his eyes and the boasting of what he has and does – comes not from the Father but from the world. The world and its desires pass away, but the man who does the will of God lives forever.'
1 John 2:15-17

Joe needs to realize that there are no innocent, objective and morally neutral people in this world. We are all sinners. <u>People are not only blind to the truth of their sinful nature but they wilfully oppose God, the message and believers at every turn.</u> Friends may say they are happy for him but that will soon change once his behaviour begins to grow increasingly godly, his faith grows and his opinions begin to affect their lives and challenge their sinful lives. That's why people who convert to Christ often face the hostility of family members who accuse them of betrayal or trying to become posh or thinking they're better than everybody else. They feel intimidated by the faith. Deep down they feel convicted of their sin. Like a cornered dog, they feel the only avenue open to them is to go on the attack.

> **STOP**
> Q: Why do you think people would behave like this? Why wouldn't people just be happy that Joe is trying to live a new life under the command of Jesus?

3X 'If the world hates you, keep in mind that **it hated me first**. If you belonged to the world, it would love you as its own. As it is, **you do not belong to the world, but I have chosen you out of the world. That is why the world hates you**.' John 15:18-19 (NIV)

> **JOE**
> What do you mean? Are you saying that my friends and family hate God? That can't be right, surely? Some of them go to church themselves. They say that they think it's a good thing but that I just shouldn't take it all so seriously.

> **STOP**
> Q: How does **John 3:19-20** help us answer Joe's questions at this point.

3X 'And this is the judgment: the light has come into the world, and people loved the darkness rather than the light because their works were evil. For everyone who does wicked things hates the light and does not come to the light, lest his works should be exposed.
John 3:19-20

Here's what Joe needs to understand about the whole of the human race, including his family and friends.

**They love the darkness rather than the light
because <u>their works are evil</u>.**

**They hate the light
because they don't want their evil <u>exposed</u>.**

In other words, his family and friends are OK with him going to church and trying to be a good person. But they don't want him to actually take his faith seriously. Why not? Because the problem unbelievers have with God is a problem of
submission

ILLUSTRATION

When I lived in the jungle of Brazil we would often have to go to the bathroom in the dark because the electricity would be down. I would take a torch with me and on one of the first occasions I could have sworn that the floor was moving. When I switched the torch on there were literally hundreds of cockroaches scurrying about the bathroom floor. As soon as I shone my torch they all dived for cover to the darkest recesses of the room or down any holes they could find.

Joe's attempts to walk in submission to the will of God for his life are showing up the sinful hearts and lives of many of his friends. They don't want that exposed so their only solution is to try and bring him down. His walking in the light only shows up the dark recesses of their hearts more clearly. <u>Their opposition to him is actually a run to cover from the light</u>. The problem is not that they disbelieve in God but that they don't want to submit to Him in any way. They are living in complete opposition to God and everything He stands for. <u>They don't want to glorify God and they definitely don't want Joe to be glorifying God either</u>.

There are two different kinds of people in the world. <u>The God haters and the God lovers</u>. That's it. There are no people who 'sit on the fence' when it comes to the Christian faith.

Christians believe that Jesus is the God-Man who came into the world to die on the cross in order to rescue guilty sinners.

The world rejects this out of hand and will find any way it can to undermine this truth.

They'll try calling Him a 'good man' or a great 'moral teacher' in order to soften the language. Failing that, they will call Him a 'fraud and a fake' or a 'lunatic and a liar'. As soon as Joe, or any other Christian start making black and white claims about God and the gospel of Jesus, they will quickly run into a wall of hostility. Don't believe me? Try these statements out on unbelieving family and friends:

> **Jesus is God.**
> **Faith in Jesus alone is the only way we can be saved.**
> **Not all world religions are the same.**
> **The Bible is the only trustworthy message from God for this world.**
> **Hell is a real place set aside for all those who refuse to bow the knee and worship Jesus as Lord and Saviour.**
> **Sex outside of marriage is sinful.**
> **Homosexuality is sinful.**

All of these are clear truths taught in the Bible and yet how many of them are explosive in our culture? How long before we are accused of homophobia or being narrow minded or becoming brainwashed? People are happy for us to believe in Jesus as long we don't really believe in anything!

Jesus warned us long ago what would happen when He came.

3X *'Do not think that I came to bring peace on the earth; I did not come to bring peace, but a sword. For I came to set a man against his father, and a daughter against her mother, and a daughter-in-law against her mother-in-law; and a man's enemies will be the members of his household.'*
Matthew 10:34-36 (NASB)

'Do you suppose that I came to grant peace on earth? I tell you, no, but rather division; for from now on five members in one household will be divided, three against two, and two against three...' **Luke 12:51-52** (NASB)

'All who desire to live godly lives in Christ Jesus will suffer persecution.' **2 Timothy 3:12** (NHEB)

> **STOP**
>
> Q: *What do you think these verses are teaching us about the results of Jesus coming? How do you think we can apply these verses to Joe's situation? How can they encourage him?*

When God saved us out of the world we immediately became enemies of those still entrapped by the devil. The hard truth is that even some of our family members could turn against us, such is their hard-heartedness and rebellion toward God and His people. What is even harder to stomach is that the watching world likes nothing better than seeing a Christian crash and burn.

The bottom line is that the world hates the Lord Jesus.

He is the light of the world and the devil is the prince of darkness.

He wants to keep people in the dark and he will do anything within his power to oppose us and the message of the good news.

That's why Jesus was killed. It's why the early disciples of Jesus were killed. It's why Christians have been killed throughout history and why Christians are murdered around the globe today. But Joe needs to understand that Jesus foresaw all of this. He warned His disciples, and all of His followers, that there could be a great cost to following Him. Joe needs the assurance that what is happening to him is not unusual.

STAND FIRM

We talked of arming ourselves with the word of God in chapter 1. But Joe, as with all Christians, must stand firm in this battle with the world. We must not be tempted to give up the fight and 'go with the flow' no matter how much pressure we come under. We must resist the temptation to give up or fold under the pressure.

PRAY

This sort of thing should always lead us to run to God in prayer. The Apostle Paul faced all sorts of hardships in his life. People were trying to kill him and undermine his faith at every point. But listen to what he says in 2 Corinthians 12:10: 'For the sake of Christ, then, I am content with weaknesses, insults, hardships, persecutions, and calamities. For when I am weak, then I am strong.' Joe, like all of us, must learn to run to Jesus when he is at his lowest.

STAY FAITHFUL TO GOD

We cannot be friends with the world and God. We cannot hope to stand by having a foot in both camps. Some Christians think they can escape persecution and mockery by keeping their heads down and being a sort of 'half and half' Christian. In other words, they go to church on Sunday, read the Bible sometimes during the week and maybe even pray. They wouldn't deny Christ but they live a completely double life the rest of the week. They go out drinking with their friends. They sleep around and they try to justify it by wanting to appear relevant. They don't want to cause ripples in their families or cause divisions among their friends. They fudge the answers to difficult questions on issues like homosexuality, abortion and marriage. But what does the Bible have to say about this?

 'You adulterous people! Do you not know that friendship with the world is enmity with God? Therefore whoever wishes to be a friend of the world makes himself an enemy of God.' **James 4:4**

Do you see how strong the language is here? <u>Friendship with the world is hatred toward God</u>. There's no escaping the harshness of that language! <u>We can be in the world or we can be in Christ</u>. We cannot be in both at the same time. <u>If we have one foot in the world, then we have one foot in the camp of the devil</u>. It is as simple as that.

 ## MEMORY VERSE

'I have said these things to you, that in me you may have peace. In the world you will have tribulation. But take heart; I have overcome the world.' (John 16:33)

SUMMARY

Joe needs to understand that the reaction of family and friends to his grow-ing faith is not unusual. Indeed, Jesus warns all of His followers to expect opposition on earth. Joe needs to stand firm, pray to the Lord, trust in Jesus and stay faithful to God. He has entered a spiritual war and the world is one of the enemies of God that he will come up against again and again.

But the fight doesn't stop there. There is another enemy Joe must face in this all out spiritual battle...

WHAT'S THE POINT?

WE CAN BE OUR OWN WORST ENEMY IN THE CHRISTIAN LIFE.

ENEMY 2:
THE FLESH

> ### JOE
> Joe is really struggling with the Christian life. He desperately wants to follow Jesus but he keeps finding himself in situations where he is sinning. He feels up one moment and then down the next. He just doesn't understand what is going on inside his head. He feels conflicted most of the time and he sometimes feels like he is losing his mind.

Here's what Joe needs to know:

Christ has already fought and won the ultimate war over sin when He went to the cross.

Death has been defeated and God's wrath has been averted.

We are born again into spiritual life when we turn to Jesus in repentance and faith.

BUT there is something within us that bursts out of us from time to time. We fight against various temptations.

Sometimes we get so angry.
Sometimes we just have to feed on the juiciest gossip.
Sometimes we feel the need to make that cruel,
backbiting jibe.
Sometimes sexual lusts dominate us.
Sometimes material greed overcomes us.
Sometimes we are blinded by selfishness.

Sometimes bitterness clouds our vision.

This is all really confusing for young and new believers like Joe who really do feel like they are losing their minds as they struggle with an internal battle that they never faced before they came to Christ. The Apostle Paul was a man who knew all about this fight. He was constantly battling against HIMSELF in the Bible.

 'We know that the law is spiritual; but I am unspiritual, sold as a slave to sin. I do not understand what I do. For what I want to do I do not do, but what I hate I do. And if I do what I do not want to do, I agree that the law is good. As it is, it is no longer I myself who do it, but it is sin living in me. For I know that good itself does not dwell in me, that is, in my sinful nature. For I have the desire to do what is good, but I cannot carry it out. For I do not do the good I want to do, but the evil I do not want to do – this I keep on doing. Now if I do what I do not want to do, it is no longer I who do it, but it is sin living in me that does it. So I find this law at work: Although I want to do good, evil is right there with me. For in my inner being I delight in God's law; but I see another law at work in me, waging war against the law of my mind and making me a prisoner of the law of sin at work within me. What a wretched man I am! Who will rescue me from this body that is subject to death? Thanks be to God, who delivers me through Jesus Christ our Lord! **Romans 7:14-25** (NIV)

Look at what Paul says in these verses.

I do not understand what I do.
    What I want to do I do not do.
      What I hate I do.
          I know good does not live in me.
          I keep on doing evil.
I want to do good but I don't.
    There is a war raging in my mind.
      What a wretch I am!

That is a man who knows something of the spiritual struggle of the Christian life! This is a man who knows what it is like to feel on top of the world one minute and in the depths of despair the next.

One of the biggest enemies we face in the Christian life is actually OURSELVES.

3✖ *'For the desires of the flesh are against the Spirit, and the desires of the Spirit are against the flesh; for these are opposed to each other, to prevent you from doing what you would.'* **Galatians 5:17**

> **STOP**
> Q: *What are these verses teaching us about the internal battle that each Christian faces?*

THE FLESH

In **Galatians 5:13** Paul warns the church about not using their freedom **to indulge the flesh**. What exactly does he mean here? He goes on in Galatians 5 to explains himself in verses 19-21: *'The acts of the flesh are obvious: sexual immorality, impurity and debauchery; idolatry and witchcraft; hatred, discord, jealousy, fits of rage, selfish ambition, dissensions, factions and envy; drunkenness, orgies, and the like. I warn you, as I did before, that those who live like this will not inherit the kingdom of God.'* (NIV)

For Paul the flesh refers to our old sinful nature.

> It is the will we inherited from Adam.
> It is the will inside our children that causes them to grow up and say no to us almost as soon as they are able to talk!
> It makes men leave their wives.
> It causes anger and rage to swell up within us.
> It causes arguments and divisions.
> It makes us want to forget church on a Sunday morning and have a lie in instead.

It makes us think that the human race isn't that bad and doesn't really need a saviour.

It makes us look to gratify and satisfy our own selfish desires as opposed to seeking out and living for the pleasure of God.

<u>The flesh, the thing that arouses all the sinful passions within us and always looks to please itself.</u>

JOE

I'm constantly battling with sin at the minute. Just when I think I have my anger under control, another sin comes up in its place. Then I seem to get that under control and the anger comes back up. I just don't seem to be able to get it together. Does that mean I won't inherit the kingdom of God?

Here's what Joe needs to know:

1. Conflict is normal in the Christian life. He is not on his own. **ALL TRUE CHRISTIANS STRUGGLE**. <u>In fact, struggle in the Christian life is one of the signs of spiritual rebirth</u>.

2. A Christian must learn to **FIGHT** these struggles in the power of the Holy Spirit. (More of this later.)

3. Conflict in our souls is not necessarily an evil thing. God can be using it for our own good. **BUT, if we find ourselves in a position where we are at peace with our sin and we are no longer fighting, then we are in BIG TROUBLE**.

3X *'For we know that our old self was crucified with him so that the body ruled by sin might be done away with, that we should no longer be slaves to sin.'* **Romans 6:6** (NIV)

'You were taught, with regard to your former way of life, to put off your old self, which is being corrupted by its deceitful desires.' **Ephesians 4:22** (NIV)

'Do not lie to each other, since you have taken off your old self with its practices.' **Colossians 3:9** (NIV)

Joe needs to understand that his old, fleshly self, is alive and kicking. <u>The old Joe doesn't want to go down without a fight</u>. **Joe wants to follow Jesus and he doesn't want to follow Jesus at the same time**. His conscience has been awakened to sin. Where once he was sleepwalking to his death, the Lord, by the power of the Holy Spirit, has woken him up to his spiritual condition. The old Joe doesn't like this. He wants to go back to sleep.

When we come to faith in Jesus the Holy Spirit <u>makes us new</u>.

We have <u>a new desire</u> to please God.
We have <u>a new desire</u> to read the Bible.
We have <u>a new desire</u> to worship with God's people.

But the old man inside of us is constantly fighting back. He doesn't want to do any of these things. The old man wants to:

Please himself.

Follow his own desires.

Hang out with the old crowd.

Therefore, <u>all Christians have to learn how to fight against that indwelling sin</u>.

> **STOP**
> Q: If all of this is true, then what do you think Christians should be doing in order to make sure the old man doesn't win over the new man on a regular occasion?

WE HAVE TO LEARN TO WALK IN THE SPIRIT

Paul's advice in **Galatians 5:16** to *'walk in the spirit'* (KJV) seems laughably simple. It sounds like a pretty impractical Christian cliché. How is that going to help us with our anger problems? How will that help us battle the pride in our lives? We want something more specific. We want some real boundaries and direction. We want some rules to keep ourselves in check. We need something to measure our progress by.

ILLUSTRATION

Let me read you some man-made rules for a Christian Bible College in America. I am sure they have been given to try and keep the 'flesh' in check. Trousers may not have pockets on the legs. They may not be frayed at the bottom. Hats may not be worn inside but may be worn outside at sporting events. White people may not shave their heads. You must not intentionally mismatch your clothes. All dresses and skirts must touch your knees when sitting. Women may not wear trousers but can wear tracksuit bottoms but only after prayers. No singing in the showers during quiet days. You must not have pictures of unmarried people demonstrating any physical contact in your dorms unless they happen to be children. You must not sing too loudly during prayer group. You may not go to a public library. Students must not loiter with a member of the opposite sex in any of the non-chaperoned areas. Dating is by permission only and handholding must be kept to one hand only unless it is necessary for specified and approved games. You must not use the word 'suck' or 'sucker' or even 'sucks'. Under no circumstances can men give their suit jackets to females whilst on a date. Perhaps the most important rule of all: you must not wipe your bogies on college property. This, apparently, is being cracked down upon.

Some of these rules are quite hilarious. Some of them, doubtless, are very wise. We scorn this sort of thing as over the top and outdated but how many of us actually try to live like this, just with different rules? Oh, we love Jesus. We'll have Jesus but we want other stuff as well. <u>Many of us try and come up with a plan to change our lives based on rule keeping</u>.

> **I am going to stop drinking.**
> **I am going to stop sleeping around.**
> **I am going to be a better parent or wife or husband.**
> **I am going to spend less time on the X-Box.**

JOE

But what does it mean to walk in the spirit? What does that look like? How do I do it?

Whatever it looks like in our lives, walking in step with the spirit must be something that requires grace, discipline, patience and endurance. <u>All the words we hate</u>. We live in a generation that wants it all fast and it wants it all now. It would be like taking a diet pill to lose weight rather than going to the gym or taking up running. We don't like waiting. We don't like suffering. We like the easy way out of life's problems. But this is not the Christian way. <u>Walking by the spirit means, at the very least, daily taking up the cross and following the Lord Jesus through all life's ups and downs</u>. We must be listening out for the Holy Sprit, **through the reading of God's Word**, and respond to Him as He prompts us in our lives. The key here is:

The word of God

 'Let the message of Christ dwell among you richly as you teach and admonish one another with all wisdom through psalms, hymns, and songs from the Spirit, singing to God with gratitude in your hearts.' **Colossians 3:16** (NIV)

<u>The more Joe dwells on God's Word and meets with God's people he will grow in strength and truth and it will become easier and easier to battle against the pull of the flesh</u>.

WE HAVE TO <u>DAILY</u> PUT TO DEATH OUR SIN

 'Put to death, therefore, whatever belongs to your earthly nature: sexual immorality, impurity, lust, evil desires and greed, which is idolatry. Because of these, the wrath of God is coming. You used to walk in these ways, in the life you once lived. But now you must also rid yourselves of all such things as these: anger, rage, malice, slander, and filthy language from your lips.' **Colossians 3:5-8** (NIV)

'Those who belong to Christ Jesus have crucified the flesh with its passions and desires.' **Galatians 5:24** (NIV)

We need to assess if there's anything more important than Christ in our lives. Repent of them. Run from them. We crucify the flesh not just by changing our behaviour but by drawing closer to Christ.

 ILLUSTRATION

Every single year weeds go through the concrete base in my back garden. I have to spend a small fortune on weed killer which does the job for a short while but soon they are back with a vengeance. I know that if I wanted to kill them outright I would have to lift my back garden path and deal with them at the root. But that is just too costly so, for now, I just live with the persistent problem.

This is how many Christians try and deal with the sins in their lives. They try to kill the works without dealing with the roots. Many Christians are weighed down by sin, depressed, guilty and weighed down with shame. They feel sorry and repent but the same sins keep popping up again and again. It seems like they just won't go away. That's why the root work needed to deal with sin has to be done in partnership with the Holy Spirit. It cannot be done any other way. We kill sin in our lives by loving God more and ourselves less. The more we love Him the more the flesh dies. The closer we stick to Jesus and His people then the further away from sin we will be.

Sin just can't live in the presence of Christ. Desire Jesus and the fruit of the Holy Spirit will naturally grow. Remember Jesus is not a set of rules to live by, He is a person to live with. If we spend time with Him then we become like Him, often without even noticing it. Life begins to change and our hearts begin to change. Here's what we need to know about Jesus:

We will never know Him enough.
We will never adore Him enough.
We will never comprehend Him sufficiently.
We can never get too close to Him.

Part of growing in Christ is understanding our true, human nature. <u>Coming to faith in Jesus does not make us perfect on earth even though we have been declared righteous in God's sight</u>. But it does mean:

<u>Dying to self.</u>
　　<u>Walking in the power of the Holy Spirit.</u>
　　　　<u>Putting sin to death daily</u>.

 **MEMORY VERSE**

'Therefore, brothers and sisters, we have an obligation—but it is not to the flesh, to live according to it. For if you live according to the flesh, you will die; but if by the Spirit you put to death the misdeeds of the body, you will live. For those who are led by the Spirit of God are the children of God.'
Romans 8:12-14 (NIV)

SUMMARY

To be a Christian means we are involved in a lifelong battle with our flesh. The old man, who loves sin, pops up in our lives almost constantly. But we must not stay in our sinful state. We must run to Jesus quickly and seek the forgiveness of God. Christian change always comes from the inside out and not the other way around. We think that if we stop doing things then we have changed but unless it is a true heart change then things will always be superficial and short lasting. We must walk in step with the Holy Spirit, stick close to Jesus and His people and die daily to our sins. It is going to be a slow and, often, painful and lifelong battle. **But we can get through it by leaning into Jesus**.

But, there's another opponent waiting in the wings to trip us up...

WHAT'S THE POINT?

WE HAVE A POWERFUL SPIRITUAL ENEMY WHO IS OUT TO DESTROY US.

ENEMY 3:
THE DEVIL

RECAP

When we are saved by Jesus we enter a lifelong spiritual war.
The whole world is hostile to the things of God.

JOE

Joe has obviously heard about the devil but he's not sure he really believes that he exists. Isn't he just a made up figure that people use to scare children into behaving themselves? He's heard stories from his friends of weird and creepy things happening and he's seen a lot of horror movies. So, he thinks that evil exists in the world but he's not convinced there's a master figure behind it all. That sounds a little bit far-fetched. *'I definitely believe in spirits though,'* he tells you. *'My family often go to have their (tarot) cards read and visit the local medium. They tell us stuff that only spirits could know. So, you can't tell me they're not real. My granddad has been in touch with us a few times through our medium. How do you explain that?'*

STOP

Q: *What do you think about Joe's view of the devil? Do you think he's just a made up figure or a real person? Explain your answer. What about his view of spirits? Do you think they are harmless? How would you explain how his dead granddad has been in touch with the family?*

1 John 5:19 tells us that the whole world lies under the power of the evil one. Consider the following verses.

- *We know that we are from God, and the whole world lies in the power of the evil one.* **1 John 5:19**
- *In their case the god of this world has blinded the minds of the unbelievers.* **2 Corinthians. 4:4**
- *...and you were dead in the trespasses and sins in which you once walked, following . . . the prince of the power of the air, the spirit that is now at work in the sons of disobedience.* **Ephesians. 2:1–2**

ILLUSTRATION

Mike Tyson was a very famous heavyweight boxer in the late eighties and he knocked out pretty much every fighter that stood in his way as he became one of the youngest ever heavyweight Champions of the world. Many think that his victories were just down to raw aggression but the truth is actually deeper than that. Mike would spend hundreds, thousands of hours studying the tape recordings of older fighters and he would watch videos of all of his opponents before he got into the ring. He did this, he claimed, so that he could study their weak points. That made them easier to knock out, he claimed. What is interesting is that the first man to knock him out was a little known journeyman boxer called Buster Douglas. Mike should have beaten him easily. But he never trained properly and he never watched one video of his opponent, who went on to win the fight. He had forgotten his own maxim: in order to defeat an opponent, we need to know an opponent.

Ephesians 6:12 says, *'For our struggle is not against flesh and blood, but against the rulers, against the authorities, against the powers of this dark world and against the spiritual forces of evil in the heavenly realms.'* (NIV) The Bible clearly says that we are not fighting against human beings, but against:

Principalities.
Powers.
Rulers of the darkness of this world.
Spiritual wickedness in high places.

Daniel 10:13 says *'But the prince of the Persian kingdom resisted me twenty-one days. Then Michael, one of the chief princes, came to help me, because I was detained there with the king of Persia."* There was a demon

*called the Prince of Persia. He appeared to have some kind of control over
a very real ancient kingdom called Persia.'*

The kingdom of the devil is organised. As we saw in the Daniel passage
above, there was a demon called the 'Prince of Persia.' Likewise, there
are demonic princes over continents, nations, cities, and towns. The Bible
says it is against them we are fighting. Their work is to make sure that the
kingdom of Jesus does not get established in their dominions. Although they
are invisible, they are real.

Joe needs to understand that the devil is as real as Jesus and as real as you and
me. Therefore, if he is to take his stand against the devil in his Christian life then
he better be aware of who his opponent is and what exactly he is capable of.

There's no doubt that we have a fascination in our culture with the spirit
world. Yet, try speaking about God and Jesus and people's eyes soon
glaze over. But, mention demons, ghosts and vampires, and suddenly their
eyes are ablaze with deep interest. This great interest in the supernatural
has seen explosive growth – in the UK at least – of witches' covens,
spiritualist churches, séances and mediums. Whilst many people happily
believe in these things, they seem less open to the Bible's view that there is
actually one person masterminding the whole thing behind the scenes. This
individual is all over the Bible and is known by many names:

The Devil (which means slanderer).
Satan (which means adversary).
The Tempter.
The Evil One.
The Ruler of the Power of the Air.
The Ruler of this World.
Beelzebub (which means lord of the flies).
The Accuser.
Addabbon (which means the one who destroys).

The sole intention of this person is to try and trip up Christians. He wants to
ruin their witness, wreck their relationships and pull them back into a sinful

and destructive lifestyle. The Bible warns us that we have to be on the look out for the devil.

 3X *'Be alert and of sober mind. Your enemy the devil prowls around like a roaring lion looking for someone to devour.'* **1 Peter 5:8** (NIV)

> **JOE**
> *If this is all true, then where did the devil come from? Who created the devil?*

The first thing we must understand is that <u>God created an angel called Lucifer</u>. The problem is that Lucifer became proud and arrogant and wanted to become like God. A prophet called **Isaiah** wrote about this long ago in **chapter 12:12-14**: *'How you have fallen from heaven, morning star, son of the dawn! You have been cast down to the earth, you who once laid low the nations! You said in your heart, "I will ascend to the heavens; I will raise my throne above the stars of God; I will sit enthroned on the mount of assembly, on the utmost heights of Mount Zaphon. I will ascend above the tops of the clouds; I will make myself like the Most High".'* (NIV)

Notice the language used about Lucifer here.

He fell from heaven.
He was cast down to the earth.
He wanted to be more powerful than God.

We don't know the exact details of what went on in heaven but it appears that this angel, Lucifer, got a bit too big for his boots and thought he could take on God in a battle for supreme power. The bottom line?

He lost.

One of the things it's important to remember when we are thinking of the devil is that <u>he is a real and personal being</u>. We see this as he interacts through the Bible.

He speaks.
He lies.

He works.
He desires.
He prowls.
He has plans.
He blinds.
He deceives.
He has a character.
He gets angry.

'You belong to your father, the devil, and you want to carry out your father's desires. He was a murderer from the beginning, not holding to the truth, for there is no truth in him. When he lies, he speaks his native language, for he is a liar and the father of lies.' **John 8:44** (NIV)

'Now is the time for judgment on this world; now the prince of this world will be driven out.' **John 12:31** (NIV)

'He must not be a recent convert, or he may become conceited and fall under the same judgment as the devil.' **1 Timothy 3:6** (NIV)

'The one who does what is sinful is of the devil, because the devil has been sinning from the beginning. The reason the Son of God appeared was to destroy the devil's work.' **1 John 3:8** (NIV)

> **STOP**
> Q: What are some the things these verses are teaching us about the character of the devil? What is he like?

> **JOE**
> This is interesting but what does this have to do with my life and my struggles?

Joe needs to understand that if he is going to win the spiritual battle against his enemy, the devil, then he needs to be aware that the devil will attack him, and all true Christians, on three fronts.

1. Satan wants to deceive us with lies.

Satan is a liar. He has been lying since the beginning. We see this in Genesis 3 when the devil lies to Eve. And his lies are very subtle. He says to Eve: *'Did God really say?'* And Satan's lies to us usually come via the mind. In 2 Corinthians 11:3 Paul reminds the church: *'But I am afraid that just as Eve was deceived by the serpent's cunning, your minds may somehow be led astray from your sincere and pure devotion to Christ.'* (NIV) The devil wants our minds to be led away from Christ and His ways. And Satan loves to twist our thoughts to move us away from Christ. <u>He wants to make us morally stupid</u>. And that's what we do when we sin. He tells us:

Just one more drink. That won't harm you…
Just one more look? What harm will it do to talk to her? Your wife will never know…
It won't matter too much if you don't bother reading your Bible today, or tomorrow…
Church isn't all that important. They won't miss you anyway…
It isn't that bad a sin. Jesus will forgive you anyway…

So how do we battle his lies? We need to <u>know</u> the word of God. We need to know what God actually says. <u>The battle against the devil's lies is always won in the mind</u>.

 'Do not be conformed to this world, but be transformed by the renewal of your mind, that by testing you may discern what is the will of God, what is good and acceptable and perfect.' **Romans 12:2**

2. Satan tempts us with our desires.

The devil and his demons knows what tempts us because they see what we watch and what we buy and what we look at. So they will tempt us in the areas that really draw us in. <u>If we struggle with sexual purity then he will tempt us specifically in this area</u>. He will throw women or men our way. He will draw your attention to the porn section of the newsagent. He will draw your attention to the porn sites online. He will bring an inappropriate relationship along your way. Time and again in the Christian life men and women have had their faith shipwrecked this way.

If we struggle with money he will tempt us to hoard and to fixate on it. The devil will tempt you through adverts and at the shops. He will whisper in our ear: *'You need that new pair of trainers. You need that new dress. Don't worry about the money, you can pay that back another time!'* And temptation leads us to our evil desires and we are drawn away from Christ. Satan longs to entangle us in sin. He wants to ruin our witness.

3X *'When tempted, no one should say, "God is tempting me." For God cannot be tempted by evil, nor does he tempt anyone; but each person is tempted when they are dragged away by their own evil desire and enticed. Then, after desire has conceived, it gives birth to sin; and sin, when it is full-grown, gives birth to death.'* **James 1:13-15** (NIV)

3. Accusations against our conscience.

The devil accuses us day and night. He likes to take us to a courtroom and remind us of our past. *'You can't be a Christian. You aren't good enough. I know what you are **really** like!'* But we need to constantly remind ourselves that Jesus has forgiven us all our sins through His blood on the cross!

3X *'There is therefore now no condemnation for those who are in Christ Jesus.'* **Romans 8:1**

He can accuse us but there is no weight behind his accusations. Just consider the wonderful truth in this verse of the hymn, *'Before the Throne.'*

> **When Satan tempts me to despair**
> **And tells me of the guilt within,**
> **Upward I look and see Him there**
> **Who made an end of all my sin.**
> **Because the sinless Saviour died**
> **My sinful soul is counted free.**
> **For God the just is satisfied**
> **To look on Him and pardon me.**

Satan is a defeated enemy.

Jesus is greater than the devil.

This is not Star Wars with two equal forces. Jesus has smashed Satan on the cross and has full authority over him. Remember that Satan is a dog on a chain but if we play with him then we will get burnt. We need to watch out for Satan's schemes but we have no need to fear him.

> **JOE**
> *This all sounds a bit heavy! How am I supposed to fight the devil? He sounds like he's far too powerful for me. How am I supposed to sleep at night knowing he is around and he is after me?*

Well, here comes the good news! In Mark's gospel chapter 1 Jesus heals a man with an evil spirit and the crowd react in v. 27 by shouting: *'What is this? A new teaching — and with authority! He even gives orders to impure spirits and they obey him.'* (NIV) We must remember that although Satan is a powerful evil being he is under God's control. Satan is nothing more than an angry dog on a chain. He's got a powerful bark and he can show his fangs but as long as we keep out of his reach then he cannot harm us.

All over the New Testament we see Jesus healing people and commanding demons to come out of people. **In fact, seven out of Jesus' thirty-five miracles were to do with casting out of demons — that's 20 per cent of all his miracles!** So, even though the devil has power, compared to Jesus it is very limited indeed. **The devil is limited in power, knowledge, authority, time and space.** The greatest victory for Jesus came at the cross. When Jesus died for our sins and was resurrected this dealt a mortal wound to the devil and his demons. They will never recover.

3X *'And having disarmed the powers and authorities, he made a public spectacle of them, triumphing over them by the cross.'* **Colossians 2:15** (NIV)

'Since the children have flesh and blood, he too shared in their humanity so that by his death he might break the power of him who holds the power of death – that is, the devil – and free those who all their lives were held in slavery by their fear of death.' **Hebrews 2:14-15** (NIV)

'And the devil, who deceived them, was thrown into the lake of burning sulphur, where the beast and the false prophet had been thrown. They will be tormented day and night for ever and ever.' **Revelation 20:10** (NIV)

> **STOP**
> Q: *What do we think these verses are teaching us about Jesus power over the devil?*

Now it's *important* to remember that not all evil and sin is from Satan and demons. Actually little in the NT is spoken about demonic activity and opposing such activity. It's really limited to the gospels and book of Acts. As we've already discovered, the Bible talks about the fact that we battle not just with Satan but with the world and the flesh. **We need to remember that we are sinful as well**.

> The devil can only tempt us.
> > He cannot <u>make</u> us do anything.
> > > We are 100 per cent *responsible* for our own actions.

MEMORY VERSE

'Little children, you are from God and have overcome them, for he who is in you is greater than he who is in the world.' **1 John 4:4**

SUMMARY

The devil and demons are real. There is a spiritual world beyond what we can see. They are a powerful and sneaky enemy. They want to lie to us, deceive us and undermine our faith.

BUT Satan and his forces are limited by the Sovereign hand of God AND very importantly have been defeated by the cross of Christ.

WHAT'S THE POINT?

WE ARE CALLED TO FIGHT AND GUARANTEED TO WIN.

FIGHTING TEMPTATION

> ## JOE
> Joe is confused. If God is stronger than the devil, then why doesn't He just help Joe out? Why does he have to be tempted all the time? At the moment Joe is feeling tempted in all sorts of areas. His drug dealers are constantly on the phone to him offering him products at rock bottom prices. Women are coming out of the woodwork and he is struggling to stay faithful to his wife. He's got the opportunity to make money from some seriously shady deals and he feels like he is going to give in at any moment. Does God have his back or not?

The first lesson Joe needs to learn is that

God is entirely Sovereign.

This means that <u>God is fully and utterly in control of absolutely everything</u>. He works all things according to His will and by His own power.

 'Our God is in the heavens; he does all that he pleases.' **Psalm 115:3**

Let's remind ourselves of what we have learned so far:

We are fighting a spiritual battle on three fronts: **the flesh, the world and the devil**.

The devil does have power but it is **not even close to being equal to God's supreme power** in any way.

The devil has **already been completely defeated** and God has demonstrated this when He went to the cross. We remind ourselves of **Colossians 2:15**: *'He disarmed the rulers and authorities and put them to open shame, by triumphing over them in him.'*

So it does beg the question, if our enemies are so defeated, what's with the war?

Even though God has ultimately defeated all His enemies, **He has chosen to not entirely remove them completely yet**. There is a future waiting for the devil that has been revealed to us in **Revelation 20:10**: *And the devil, who deceived them, was thrown into the lake of burning sulphur, where the beast and the false prophet had been thrown. They will be tormented day and night for ever and ever.* (NIV)

This means that God, in His great wisdom, has fixed a day for His enemies when they will be fully and finally brought to their knees and great ruin. Until then, He has guaranteed that they can cause mischief and trouble but they will not win the final victory against Him or His people.

Whatever the devil does to the church **he cannot stop the advance of the kingdom of God**. Whatever the devil does to try to trip us up **he cannot stop the advance of the work of God in our lives**. Whatever difficulties we go through now, there will come a day when God will get all the glory. Therefore, Joe, like all true Christians, must live in this world as an advertisement for the future reality. As Christians faithfully wage war and resist evil they act like megaphones of the glory of God to the watching world. Every triumph over the world, the flesh and the devil shouts out loud and clear that living for God is more important than sinful pleasure. When we resist temptation we pronounce judgment on all wickedness. When we give in to temptation we are advertising the enemy and his tactics – we are denying the truth that God is good and glorious. When we give in to temptation we are saying that the pleasures of this life are worth more than the treasures of the next.

ILLUSTRATION

I love watching spy movies. They are notorious for the many plot turns and twists along the storytelling process. You usually are on the edge of your seat for these films as you follow these incredibly gifted people in very difficult circumstances trying to uncover secrets from some villainous empire in an effort to save the world. One particularly riveting kind of spy movie is the ones involving the double agent. These are the stories where you are rooting for a spy and their work, only to find out that at some point the spy had been turned into a double agent. They are actually found to be working for who they were supposed to be working against!

This is what God's enemies seek to do with temptations.

They seek to make Christians renounce the faith;

first in
action
and
then in belief.

With each carefully placed temptation God's enemies are seeking to have us switch teams. They want us to leave God, and go back to our old way of life. That is the end of all temptations our enemies thrust in our way; they seek through temptation to get us to say, through disobedience, that God is not as good as He is — that sin brings more joy than God, Himself.

> **STOP**
> Q: What are temptations? What do they look like in your life? What are some of the things/habits that you know are bad for you, yet you struggle to say no?

Now, Joe knew about temptations **before he came to Jesus**. He knew what it was like to face that internal battle of trying to stop doing something he knew was wrong or harmful.

He wanted to stop drug dealing.
 He wanted to stop sleeping around.
  He wanted to stop stealing cars.

But it just seemed like he didn't have the power to say no.

Now that he is walking with the Lord, he's concerned that he will be just as powerless against those temptations. Well, in the Christian life temptations are certainly an ever present reality. They never go away. As we have said, there are forces opposed to us being reconciled with God. There are enemies who would seek to have us reject God and turn away from Jesus. And one way this opposition presents itself is through temptations.

But, what exactly is a temptation? Temptations usually don't come with a neon flashing sign saying, *'temptation'.* They come disguised as a friend to our feelings, but truly they are enemies to our faith. A temptation is something that tries us. It tests our allegiance to Jesus and our willingness to sin against Him. In other words, a temptation is something that causes us to consider choosing anything over Jesus. For instance, a temptation can come from a situation that invites someone to enjoy the moments of sexual sin, against having self-control and pleasing God. Perhaps it's a temptation to escape some not-too-pleasant consequences by lying, rather than just telling the truth and trusting that God will do right by us no matter what the consequences are. As varied as sin is, so are the different ways temptations present themselves. But make no mistake, they all have the same end in view.

To get someone to choose living in sin over living by faith.

Temptations seek to elevate **what the eyes see** over and above **faith in what God says**. In the beginning, we see the Devil using this tactic as he tempted Eve to sin against God, He said to the woman in **Genesis 3:1**, *'Did God actually say, "You shall not eat of any tree in the garden"?'* Now where was the temptation? It was in encouraging her to question God. She knew what God had said, but she was before a beautiful delicious-looking tree. Rather than trust God's word by faith, she chose to go with what she could see. Look at **Genesis 3:6**, *'So when the woman saw that the tree* *was good for food, and that it was a delight to the eyes, and that the tree was to be desired to make one wise, she took of its fruit and ate, and she also gave some to her husband who was with her, and he ate.'* She didn't fight this temptation, but gave in to it. <u>Obedience was abandoned, and sin was preferred</u>. What was an opportunity for her to fight the temptation and show how good God's word is, turned into a fall into disobedience and a feast of sin and death.

<u>These kinds of fights are before us all</u>. There are thousands of moments weekly where we are tempted to abandon faith in what God has said in exchange for sin more pleasing to what we can see. Christians are those who live by faith. We don't live by faith perfectly, but we do live by faith. We are committed to resisting temptations to sin and pursuing the things that please God. As **Hebrews 10:39** puts it, *'But we are not of those who shrink back and are destroyed, but of those who have faith and preserve their souls.'*

JOE

So, I know that temptations come from the world, the devil and the flesh? But how do I know if and when I am being tempted? What does temptation look like?

'Blessed is the one who perseveres under trial because, having stood the test, that person will receive the crown of life that the Lord has promised to those who love him. When tempted, no one should say, "God is tempting me." For <u>God cannot be tempted by evil, nor does he tempt anyone</u>; but each person is tempted when they are dragged away by their own evil desire and enticed. Then, after desire has conceived, it gives birth to sin; and sin, when it is full-grown, gives birth to death.' **James 1:12-15** (NIV)

Here's what we learn first from these verses. Temptations **DO NOT** come from God. <u>God is not like our enemies</u>. <u>God is after our good</u>. In fact, God uses the temptations and trials in our lives so that our faith can grow and we become spiritually stronger.

3X *'In all this you greatly rejoice, though now for a little while you may have had to suffer grief in all kinds of trials. These have come so that the proven genuineness of your faith – of greater worth than gold, which perishes even though refined by fire – may result in praise, glory and honour when Jesus Christ is revealed.'* **1 Peter 1:6-7** (NIV)

God is not trying to trip us up in our temptations. In fact, the Bible is clear that we often trip ourselves up, as well as the devil, the flesh and the world. Look closely at **James 1:12-15** and you will see the <u>clear steps that lead us from temptation to sin</u>.

1. A thought pops into our brain.

Maybe it's a pretty girl walking down the street.
Maybe a dealer offers us some good product for a cheap price.
Maybe we are tempted to tell a lie to cover up something we did.
Maybe we are enticed by just 'one more drink'.
Maybe we hear a juicy bit of gossip about somebody and we have the urge to add fuel to the fire.
Maybe we are out at the shops and we see a pair of shoes that are out of budget and will put us in debt.
Maybe we are online and a porn site advert pops up.

These things, and more, can <u>pop into our brain for only the briefest second</u>. Sometimes it is just a fleeting thought. Often it is an emotion:

Lust.
Anger.
Immorality.
Covetousness (wanting something that's not yours).
Drunkenness.
Indulgence.

<u>At this point no sin has been committed</u>. But the warning light has flashed on.

2. The thought swirls around in our brain.

Now we're not just looking at the girl, we are fantasising about her.
> **We're not just thinking about using, we are playing the 'rush' it would give us over and over in our mind.**
> *We're not just thinking about the person who has annoyed us, we are playing their destruction in our mind.*

We're not just thinking of a lie, we're thinking of lies to cover the lie.

And on and on. Playing with the thoughts. Toying with the emotions. We are walking down a dangerous path at this point.

3. We decide to sin.

Sin is a choice. We make a decision to disobey God ultimately because that is what we want to do. We might try to excuse ourselves but it does not change the fact that we made a decision to sin.

> *'I couldn't help myself.'*
> *'I didn't mean to.'*
> *'I didn't plan it. It just happened.'*
> *'They made me angry.'*

All these excuses, and more, are lies of the devil. **Every time we give in to temptation and sin we do it knowingly and consciously.** When our thoughts become actions, sin is made alive in us. <u>We have now crossed a line.</u>

4. We act out our sin.

We take that drink.
We take those drugs.
We buy what we can't afford.
We lie.
We steal.
We cheat with that girl.
We hurt other people.

We click on that porn pop up.

We have opened the door for the Devil to come into our lives and wreak havoc. Our sin is now *'out there'*.

5. Our sin becomes full grown.

One drink too many has turned into a three-day bender.

A quick click on the wrong internet site has turned into a two-hour trawl through filth.

Buying those shoes has turned into maxing out your credit card, with no hope of repayment.

A little lie has turned into telling more and more to cover ourselves.

Exchanging Facebook messages with a girl has turned into a sexual encounter.

Having angry thoughts about somebody has turned into violence.

Once we open the door to indulge our lusts and desires, it is hard to close it again. We get swarmed with feelings of guilt and shame but we still carry on regardless. For those of us whose particular sin is chemical and/or gambling (usually they go hand in hand) then it does not take long for our sin to turn into a full blown addiction. The longer we go on, the further we get from the cross and the harder it is to stop.

6. We have to face the consequences of our sin.

Sin always, and only, leads to one conclusion: **death**. For the sinner who refuses to repent it is an eternal, physical separation from God in hell. The Apostle Paul is clear in **Romans 6:23** that the wages of sin is death. Even as Christians we must not be fooled into thinking that there will be no consequences for our sinful actions.

Every drug high has a come down period. The consequences are going to be debt, ill health and, long term, mental health issues.

Every shopping spree leads to bills that must be paid. Sometimes that leads to bailiffs and often leads to the breakdown of relationships.

Every violent act has consequences. It can lead to pain, death and trauma.

<u>The more we engage in sinful activities the further into the darkness we stumble</u>. The more we give in to temptation the more negative consequences begin to appear in our lives.

We feel guilt.
    We become hard hearted.
        We become bitter.
            We become angry.
                We become deceitful.
                    We become depressed.
                        We become suicidal.
                            We feel powerless to change.
                              We hurt our families, our friends and ourselves.

The only answer to temptation is to fight it. To fight it at the point of entry. To kick it out of our minds before we begin to go down a path we will ultimately regret. God has called us not only to fight but to endure; to remain strong in our faith through temptations. We must not buckle under their weight and give in. Paul reminds the church in **1 Corinthians 10:13**: *'No temptation has overtaken you that is not common to man. God is faithful, and he will not let you be tempted beyond your ability, but with the temptation he will also provide the way of escape, that you may be able to endure it.'* In other words, God is faithful to give us all the help we need to endure temptation.

 MEMORY VERSE

'Therefore, my beloved, as you have always obeyed, so now, not only as in my presence but much more in my absence, work out your own salvation with fear and trembling, for it is God who works in you, both to will and to work for his good pleasure.' **Philippians 2:12-13**

SUMMARY

Temptations seeks to lead us away from faith in God's Word and take us into sin. But God has given us His Spirit and equipped us with weapons to help us in our fight against temptation. God won His victory and He helps us to win against temptation as well.

> **STOP**
>
> Q: So, the question is: how does Joe win in his war against the world, the flesh and the devil? How is he going to fight against the continual assault of temptations in his life? What does he need to do to fight against his sin and endure?

Let's find out....

WHAT'S THE POINT?

WE NEED A PLAN TO FIGHT AGAINST OUR SPIRITUAL ENEMIES IN THIS WORLD.

HAVING A
BATTLE PLAN

RECAP

When we are saved by Jesus we enter a lifelong spiritual war.
The whole world is hostile to the things of God.
We have a powerful spiritual enemy who is out to destroy us.
We are called to fight and guaranteed to win.

JOE

Joe's emotions are all over the place. To be honest his head is in a spin with all this talk of spiritual warfare and the world, the flesh and the devil. His life seems to have become more complicated since he became a Christian and now he has to put up with an almost endless stream of temptations. Just when he thinks he has overcome one area of struggle another one comes up. Of course he realises that God is all powerful and has his back but that information doesn't seem to help him in the heat of battle. He's come to you for help.

ILLUSTRATION

Soldiers who have fought in battles say that when bullets start flying the mind goes blank and switches to autopilot. This is where proper training is of paramount importance. Soldiers cannot be expected to be effective in battle if they have been shown something only once. They must be drilled in military skills until those skills become second nature. Then when the bullets start flying, trained soldiers will automatically respond with the appropriate action or manoeuvre without conscious thought of what should be done.

When we are in the middle of a spiritual war we need to remember our training and we need to have a battle plan. This is what is going to help us deal with temptation and the ever present threat of sin in our lives. But soldiers on the ground will almost always have to call in air support when the going gets tough. Thankfully, in Jesus, God has provided all the air support we need in our spiritual battles.

3X *'...and his incomparably great power for us who believe. That power is the same as the mighty strength he exerted when he raised Christ from the dead and seated him at his right hand in the heavenly realms.'* **Ephesians 1:19-20** (NIV)

Let those verses sink in! The Christian has complete access to the same power that **raised Christ from the dead**. That is more powerful than any weapon on planet earth and it is completely at our disposal. **We can call down the greatest air support in the history of the world to help us when times get tough**. That's why we should not be afraid of fighting this war. We are called and equipped to be soldiers of Christ. God has given us everything we need to win; he has assured us of victory, and those who overcome shall reign with Jesus forever.

But how exactly do we do it? How do we fight temptation? Well ask any Christian who has been walking with Jesus for a while, and they will tell you there are many ways to fight temptation. But let's consider the following verses and use them as the basis for our battle plan.

3X *'Submit yourselves, then, to God. Resist the devil, and he will flee from you. Come near to God and he will come near to you.'* **James 4:7-8a** (NIV)

1. Submit to God.

Notice, first of all we are commanded to submit to God. We are to bow to His authority in every area of our life. James says we are to put ourselves under the command of God. What is submission? The word submit is connected to enlisting. We are signing up to fight with the Lord. It is setting aside your will for your life and handing it over to God. It is saying to God, *'I am yours, do what you like with me'*. Paul tells us to submit to one another in Ephesians. Wives are told to submit to husbands. We are all told to submit to our leaders. And yet most of us don't want to do it. We've all got reasons why we don't like to submit. We want to be the boss of our own lives. Some of us do it grudgingly. OK, then, if I have to.

ILLUSTRATION

When my children were younger we used to make them put away their toys before they went to bed. Almost without exception they begged me to let them carry on playing for 'five more minutes'. Then, when the time came to do what I asked they would huff and puff and make a real scene doing it. They would drag their heels and take as long as they possibly could. They knew they had to obey me so they did just enough to try my patience but not so far as to be called disobedient. We called it 'skirting the edge'.

That's how many Christians act around the issue of submission. Some of us look like we submit on the outside but inside we are seething. We are raging. We are doing it grudgingly. We are *'skirting the edge'*. That is not biblical submission. If a wife is nagging she is not submissive to God. If a husband is unloving and critical he is not submitting to God. If we find the commands of God tiresome and irritating, then we are not submitting to God. <u>We find out how truly we are submitting to God when we have to do something we don't want to</u>. It's OK singing about it on Sundays but what happens on Monday when God asks us to do something that we don't want to do? <u>There is nothing uglier than joyless submission</u>. **We must submit to the Lord cheerfully**. A person who says, *'I follow Jesus'* but doesn't submit to God is a liar and the truth is not in them. <u>We cannot be saved without 100 per cent submission to God</u>. It is as simple as that. This is what a Christian is. Somebody who has wilfully and joyfully submitted their lives to the Lordship of Jesus.

So, when that moment of temptation comes we must ask ourselves, *'Is what I am about to do an act of submitting to God or an act of rebellion against him?'*

> **If you're not sure then don't do it.**
> **If you know it's wrong, then don't do it.**

<u>Submit yourself to God</u>.

2. Resist the devil.

Secondly, **James 4:7** tells us to resist the devil. We are to quite literally take our stand against him. Instead of just giving in to our selfish desires we are required **to make an effort** in the relationship. Many of us fall into sin because **we can't be bothered** to make the effort. We just run headlong into our sin. But a truly humble life that is blessed by God is marked by submission to God and resisting the devil.

ILLUSTRATION

During WWII much of France was occupied by enemy soldiers. But even though the country had been defeated there were still pockets of resistance fighters around the country that engaged in guerilla warfare with their occupiers. They would engage in smash and grab raids at night and cause as much damage as possible before running away. They couldn't hope to beat the enemy but they could cause as much irritation as possible in an effort to hinder them at every turn.

Likewise, when we come to Jesus we enter into open warfare. We are not like the French resistance because in Christ we have won the war against the devil. It is the devil and his demonic horde who are using these tactics against us. The devil will do anything and use any trick to try and trip us up and upset our faith and witness. But we must resist these attacks. Yes, it's hard but we have to do it. **We resist the devil by not resisting the work of God in our lives**. Resist means we have to be prepared to fight the devil, not give in at the first sight of the enemy. Many a war has been fought when men have turned and run on the battlefield. We cannot do that in the Christian life. And here comes the promise. The guarantee. Once we submit to God and resist the devil then **he will flee from us**. Keep fighting and resisting at every turn.

3. Come near to God.

In **John 17:3** we read, 'Now this is eternal life: that they know you, the only true God, and Jesus Christ, whom you have sent'. (NIV) The great news here is that God wants to **know us** and be known **by us**. In **Deuteronomy 4:7** we read, 'What other nation is so great as to have their gods near them the way the Lord our God is near us whenever we pray to him?' (NIV)

JOE
How do we come near to God? What does that mean? That sounds a bit weird.

It's not really strange. In fact, it is quite simple. <u>We have to make the effort to spend the time with him.</u> Many Christians don't feel near to him because they have forgotten the basic steps of living the Christian life.

READING AND MEMORISING THE BIBLE

In Matthew 4 Jesus was tempted by the devil in the wilderness with all sorts of goodies if He would only give up His plan to go to the cross. But in His moment of greatest temptation Jesus responded time and again by quoting the words of scripture. (<u>It is worth reading Mathew 4:1-11 at some point.</u>)

'I have stored up your word in my heart, that I might not sin against you.'
Psalm 119:11

When the devil comes knocking or you are feeling really tempted there is no stronger weapon than to be able to quote scripture from memory. It really is a great tool in the Christian armoury.

PRAYER

This is the big one! Jesus encouraged his disciples and, through them, us with these words in **Matthew 26:41**, *'Watch and pray that you may not enter into temptation. The spirit indeed is willing, but the flesh is weak.'*

> **We need to pray so that we won't be tempted.**
> **We need to pray during times of temptation.**

We need God's help and are encouraged to come boldly to His throne to receive mercy and find grace to help in our times of need. This is how we should pray (<u>pay careful attention to the last two lines</u>).

3 *'This, then, is how you should pray:*
> *"Our Father in heaven,*
>> *hallowed be your name,*
>> *your kingdom come,*
>> *your will be done,*
>> *on earth as it is in heaven.*
> *Give us today our daily bread.*
> *And forgive us our debts,*
>> *as we also have forgiven our debtors.*
> *And lead us not into temptation,*
>> *but deliver us from the evil one."'*

If you don't know what to pray, then this is a great place to start. It is an even better set of verses to memorise!

> ### JOE
> *I try to do these sorts of things but I'm just 'not feeling it'. I still seem to get dragged down in temptations. Maybe this sort of stuff just doesn't work for me!*

If Joe is not *'feeling it'* (by that he means close to God) then he's not doing it. Simple as that. How do we think our relationships would work if we didn't speak to our partners from one day to the next? Do we think that would help us to grow closer or would we become more distant? What if we only spoke to them once a week on a Sunday and only when other people were watching?

Or, how do we grow flowers? We care for them. We water them. They grow. What if we didn't water them or feed them or look after them? They may live for a time but sooner or later they will shrivel up and die. This is what Joe must watch out for. <u>We can all bloom in the beginning but, if we're not careful, the passage of time, the world, the flesh, the devil, temptations and failures in the battlefield mean that our faith could wither and die to almost nothing.</u>

<u>How do we think we can grow in the things of God if we can't be bothered to put the work in?</u>

Joe needs to know <u>that these disciplines do work! He has to keep persisting</u> (more of this later).

ILLUSTRATION

I do quite a lot of marriage counselling and I run into all sorts of issues with couples.

> 'We don't feel as close as we used to when we first got married.'
> 'The fun has gone.'
> 'The love has gone.'
> 'The trust has gone.'
> 'I feel cold towards her/him.'

Always my first question is: **are you communicating with one another?** And by that I don't mean arguing. **Are you talking daily? Are you listening to one another? Are you taking time to cultivate the relationship?** Almost always the answers fall into one of the following categories.

> 'No. Not really.'
> 'Not as much as we know we should.'
> 'We just can't seem to find the time.'
> 'Not since the children came along.'
> 'I/he/she works long hours.'

Love <u>must</u> be cultivated. A close relationship <u>must</u> be worked at. It does not come naturally. It is the same with the Lord. <u>He draws near to us as we draw near to Him</u>. If we neglect Him then of course He feels far away (even though in reality, He isn't).

4. RUN from sin!

<u>As we submit to God, resist the devil and come near to God we had better be doing it while running from sin!</u> These battle plans are all irrelevant if we are still giving in to temptation and running after our sin(s). We need to

Get rid of ALL of the things that seem to encourage us to sin regularly.

JOE

How far should I go in getting rid of things that are encouraging me to indulge in my sinful desires? Should I get rid of my TV or my phone? What about my Facebook page? That seems a bit hard-line doesn't it? Am I supposed to stop hanging out with the guys?

Well, let's take a look at what Jesus has to say about how far we should go in our war against sin.

'If your right eye causes you to sin, tear it out and throw it away. For it is better that you lose one of your members than that your whole body be thrown into hell. And if your right hand causes you to sin, cut it off and throw it away. For it is better that you lose one of your members than that your whole body go into hell.' **Matthew 5:29-30**

STOP

Q: In the light of these verses what is your answer to Joe's questions now?

Everybody is different and faces different trials and temptations. The point is that we must work hard to **kill the sin in our lives**. When we effectively resist temptation we are killing sin. It is no surprise that after Paul encourages the Christians in **Colossians**, he calls them to action against sin in chapter **3:4-5**. *'When Christ who is your life appears, then you also will appear with him in glory.* <u>Put to death therefore what is earthly in you</u>...'

5. Don't go it alone.

The devil has a sneaky ploy and it is <u>to isolate you at all costs</u>. That's why we really need other Christians to help us out. Not only to encourage us to fight temptation, but also to correct us when we don't. We need close brothers and sisters who can help keep us alive in the battle.

'Take care, brothers, lest there be in any of you an evil, unbelieving heart, leading you to fall away from the living God. But exhort one another every day, as long as it is called "today," that none of you may be hardened by the deceitfulness of sin. For we have come to share in Christ, if indeed we hold our original confidence firm to the end.' **Hebrews. 3:12-14**, *also ref.* **Galatians 6:1-2**

The local church is the key to our survival (more about this later in our series). It is there we will meet with others who are also in the battle with us. More mature Christians will have faced trials and temptations Joe hasn't even dreamed about. That's why it is important that Joe, as with all believers (young and old) have a spiritual mentor who can keep them accountable and walk with them through the trials of life.

 ## MEMORY VERSE

'Submit yourselves, then, to God. Resist the devil, and he will flee from you. Come near to God and he will come near to you.' **James 4:7-8a** (NIV)

SUMMARY

In order to defeat temptation and the plans of the devil, every Christian needs a battle plan. We need to realise from the start that we have all the power we need at our disposal once we are trusting in Jesus. We have nothing to fear from the enemies that plague us but we do have to be on our guard. We need to submit to God's authority, resist the devil, come near to God, RUN from sin and make sure we are in a good Christian community. That will give us the best chance for survival in the long run.

The problem is, Joe keeps on falling into temptation and sinning. What now?

WHAT'S THE POINT?

THIS SIDE OF GLORY, FAILING WILL BE A NORMAL PART OF EVERY CHRISTIAN'S LIFE.

WHAT TO DO
WHEN WE FALL

JOE

Joe is feeling a bit low. After everything he has learned about temptation and falling into sin it seems like he is failing time and time again. He thought he'd kicked his Heroin habit but after an argument with his cousin he was so angry he went and got high with some old friends. Some of them were laughing at him and questioning whether he really is a Christian after all. He's full of guilt and shame and doesn't know what to do.

STOP

Q: What would you say to Joe to try and encourage him? Do you think he really is a Christian? If so, why? If not, why not?

Everyone knows the frustration of unmet expectations. We all know what it's like to have really 'high hopes' and lofty dreams only for those dreams and plans to come crashing to the ground. Even in the book of **Proverbs 13:12** we are told, 'Hope deferred makes the heart sick, but a desire fulfilled is a tree of life.' In other words, **anytime our plans don't work out the way we thought they would, we are generally discouraged**.

Now, <u>the discouragement level is different depending on the expectation</u>.

Most of us know the frustration of pouring out a bowl of cereal only to find out that the milk is totally gone! That would be an example of a mild disappointment. But what about when you lose a job unexpectedly? That kind of surprise brings with it a discouragement level of a much greater degree.

So depending on the unexpected disappointment, discouragement levels could range from mild frustrations all the way to flat out despair. <u>Christians, however, are encouraged to not lose heart even when we feel at a great loss</u>. The Apostle Paul knew great difficulty in his life but listen to what he wrote in **2 Corinthians 4:8**, *'We are hard pressed on every side, but not crushed; perplexed, but not in despair.'* (NIV)

Joe, like all Christians, experiences the biggest discouragements when he fails to fight temptation. <u>The highest moments of Joe's discouragement come when he commits sin</u>.

One thing Joe must learn is that:

> **Perfection, though promised to Christians in glory, isn't possible this side of heaven.**

ILLUSTRATION

I remember being single and desperately wanting to be married. I read a lot of books about it and even listened to good Bible teaching about the subject so that I would be prepared if God ever gave me a spouse. But, no matter how hard I tried to prepare for marriage, I still wasn't married. The only true way to be truly married is to actually get married! Reading, studying and learning about marriage doesn't make you married. Only getting married makes you married!

So it is with living a sinless life on earth. We can do our best to not sin now in order to prepare ourselves for the sinless glory of the life to come. We can read lots of books, listen to wise counsel and hear many thousands of sermons, but <u>we will never truly be without sin until we get to heaven</u>. The following verses are going to help us think this through in a little more detail.

'For all have sinned and fall short of the glory of God, and all are <u>justified freely by his grace through the redemption that came by Christ Jesus.'</u> **Romans 3:23-24** (NIV)

'For those God foreknew he also predestined to be conformed to the image of his Son, that he might be the firstborn among many brothers and sisters. And those he predestined, he also called; those he called, he also justified; those he justified, he also glorified.' **Romans 8:29-30** (NIV)

These verses seem like a bit of a handful so let's break them down. Think of the road to heaven marked by three major road signs.

Sign 1: Justification
This word simply means that **the moment we came to faith in Jesus Christ**

God pronounced us not guilty in his sight.

When people repent of their sins and put their faith in Jesus as their only hope for eternal life God justifies them – they are forgiven of all their sins. He counts them as righteous in his sight **because of the righteousness of Jesus**. That is justification. For the Christian this has already happened. It is finished. We are justified by God once for all. **Justification is in the past**.

Sign 2: Sanctification
Sanctification is the progress we make in this life as we grow to become more and more like Jesus. Think of it as the continual work of God **through us** producing hard effort **by us** in God's strength that He **gives us**. Remember the memory verse from chapter 5? Here it is again. **Philippians 2:13**, *'For it is God who works in you, both to will and to work for his good pleasure.'* What is God's will? To work in us so that we would become more and more like His sinless son Jesus. This is our present reality. **Sanctification is a lifelong process**.

Sign 3: Glorification
Glorification then, is the end goal. It is when the Christian becomes the finished product. It is when we will enter into the presence of God where we will sin no more. When God saved us from our sins, He promised to one day conform us to the image of Jesus. So Paul, writing in **Philippians 1:6**, could say confidently, *'I am sure of this, that he who began a good work in you will bring it to completion at the day of Jesus Christ.'* Glorification

is a future reality for every Christian. **Glorification is something we are working towards**.

Put them all together and it works out like this.

> Our justification has already happened.
>> Our glorification is in the future.

Therefore,

> We live now in the era of sanctification.

The process of fighting sin in our lives now as we seek to become more like Jesus helps us to grow more and more into the image of Jesus. But just because we are working towards being like Jesus, this doesn't mean we will get to experience being made completely into His image **this side of heaven**. We will not know sinless perfection until after our death and entrance into the presence of God. It is not until after the resurrection that we get to experience the fulness of what it means to be made fully into Christ's image.

What's the point of all this? Simple. No matter how hard we try, as long as we are in this body, we will keep sinning.

Joe thinks that he is the only person in the church who keeps on sinning and letting the Lord, and himself, down. But he is wrong.

All Christians sin.
All Christians let the Lord down.

We are called to try hard, to work out our salvation – to show ourselves to be genuine Christians. But we are not able to be perfectly holy. We still sin. We still show we are in need of sanctification, we are in need of God's grace still and we long for glory more and more with each day.

So what are we to do? What should Joe do when he falls into sin?

(1) Always remember the gospel

Some people think that the gospel is just the message that gets people saved from their sin when, in reality, we learn that the gospel is what keeps and sustains Christians as well. <u>The gospel is needed wherever sin lives</u>. And as long as Christians live with a sinful nature (remember the chapter on the flesh), we will need the gospel. **We never leave the gospel.** <u>Joe needs to always be preaching the gospel to himself</u>. Joe needs to be more mindful of the grace of God in Christ than the sin and failure in himself. One old preacher put it this way, *'For every look at self, take ten looks at Christ.'* As often as he lives, everyday, he will show that he is a sinner. And as often as he lives, everyday, he should show that Jesus Christ died for sinners.

 'The saying is trustworthy and deserving of full acceptance, that Christ Jesus came into the world to save sinners...' **1 Timothy 1:15**

<u>Every time we fall, we are reminding ourselves that we are not good enough for God</u>. We know that God is holy, He is truly perfect — even now! And we have chosen, and keep choosing, to do things that grieve God and that lie about His character. While the wages of sin is death, we who have not put our confidence in ourselves but have put all our trust and confidence in Christ have been **permanently pardoned from all our sin!**

It is because of God's rich mercy and great love that we are alive in Christ. It is all of grace! That's what Paul tells the church in **Ephesians 2:8**, when he reminds them, *'For by grace you have been saved through faith. And this is not your own doing; it is the gift of God'.* So, when we fail we **look to the cross where Jesus died for our sin**. We consider the resurrection where God demonstrated for all time that **our sin debt (past, present and future) is fully paid** for and pardoned — and we are promised newness of life now. So the good news is that **Joe can be confident that God still loves him, and he can more urgently long for the day when he will be free from sinning in glory**.

(2) Keep reading the Bible.

ILLUSTRATION

Have you ever tried watching a 3D movie without the special glasses on? If we don't have them, our eyes hurt from looking at a harsh image, and the pictures on the screen seem out of focus. But once we put the glasses on everything comes back into focus. The picture on the screen looks clearer and we can begin to enjoy the film and all of its special effects. Those glasses help us to see everything more clearly.

This is how the Bible works. The Bible provides us with the glasses to view our sin and the future glory that awaits us. When we rightly look through the Word of God, we see these two realities from an eternal perspective. And with these Bible glasses we see that while every Christian still falls and sins, every Christian's future is beautifully glorious and will one day be without sin.

(3) Keep trusting God.

God knows everything. Remember when

He called us,
> **He** justified us and
>> **He was fully aware** of everything that happened in our past. But we also know that since

He promises to fully complete every Christian in Christ's image,
He knows everything that will happen through our sanctification process, and even what follows our glorification, too!
Therefore, knowing that, **we shouldn't act as if God is emotionally unstable and will cast us to the side if we sin one more time**.

God knew all the ways you were going to fall in your entire life when He justified you!
God will not abandon us even when we fall into sin.

Consider the following passage from **Luke 22:31-34**. Here, Jesus communicates with Peter about his future sin. *'Simon, Simon, behold, Satan demanded to have you, that he might sift you like wheat, but I have prayed* *for you that your faith may not fail. And when you have turned again, strengthen your brothers.'* Peter said to him, *'Lord, I am ready to go with you both to prison and to death.'* Jesus said, *'I tell you, Peter, the rooster will not crow this day, until you deny three times that you know me.'* Here's the thing. Peter was telling Jesus that he would follow him to jail and was willing to go all the way for him. But Jesus knew differently.

<u>Jesus knew not only that Peter would fail, but the specific way in which he would</u>. We know from **Luke 22:54-62** that Jesus was 100 per cent correct about Peter's sin. Peter was so quick to say he would never deny Jesus and yet as soon as Jesus is arrested and put on trial Peter is the coward hiding in the temple courtyard denying that he ever knew this man Jesus. Peter would go on to betray Jesus in a shocking way.

But what is really encouraging is that **Jesus loved Peter despite knowing he would fail**. What an encouragement for us in our darkest times! Even more, Jesus **knew** that Peter was going to repent, return to him and use his failings to encourage the church. Not only was Peter a tremendous source of encouragement to the early church, he encourages all Christians to this day. He was the guy who wrote **1 Peter 5:8-9** out of his own personal experience. *'Be sober-minded; be watchful. Your adversary the devil prowls around like a roaring lion, seeking someone to devour. Resist him, firm in your faith, knowing that the same kinds of suffering are being experienced by your brotherhood throughout the world.'*

Isn't it an encouragement to know that this wasn't written by a perfect man, though it is wisdom from a perfect God?

So, not only does God not abandon us because we fail, He has even given us a promise that He will still be working all things together for our good when we fail! This means that God can make good fruit come even from our failures — even like He did with Peter.

To help us get our minds around it, here are just a couple of good things that God brings from our failures. Three main fruits that failing produces in the lives of Christians are: **humility, our hope of glory** and a **deeper love for Christ**.

(1) Humility.

Unfortunately, even as Christians <u>we all struggle with being self-righteous</u>. Self-righteousness is a confidence in our self, when we think that we are good enough for God. It is entirely self-deception. That's what Paul tells the church in **Galatians 6:3**, *'For if anyone thinks he is something, when he is nothing, <u>he deceives himself</u>.'* The gospel totally crushes all of our **self-righteousness**. How? Because it reminds us that:

> Salvation is entirely a gift from God,
>> And it is not a result of our works or our effort, so that no one can boast.

<u>Self-righteousness means we will often see the sin in others but not in ourselves</u>.

<u>Self-righteousness means we will scorn a brother or sister when they fall but not ourselves</u>.

But self-righteousness can quickly turn into **self-glorification**. What is that?

<u>Self-glorification happens when we resist a particular temptation to sin and we put it down to our own effort and not the Holy Spirit of God</u>.

<u>Self-glorification happens when a brother or sister commits a terrible sin which we haven't committed and so we make ourselves seem morally superior to them</u>.

Self-righteousness and self-glorification are wicked sins. Therefore, what we need is an attitude of humility as we realise that our relationship with God is entirely based on **His grace and not our goodness**. If it was based on our goodness no one would have a relationship with God. This should make us <u>humble</u> and <u>grateful</u>.

> **Humble** that God would love us despite us.
>> **Grateful** that He provides everything we need for eternal life and sustains all the way to glory.

(2) We should long for heaven.

Falling into sin *should* make us more earnestly hope for the glory of heaven. <u>Every time we sin we should grieve over it</u>.

But we are not those who grieve without hope.

Our grief is different. We grieve and long for the time when we don't have to fight these battles against the flesh, the world and devil. When we can be with the Lord in eternal glory.

<u>Since glory is the place where no sin is, we long to be in that place</u>.
  <u>Since glorification is the state where we sin no more — we long more deeply for that state</u>.

There is a coming day when we will no longer sin against the Lord; in glory we will never fail Him again. And when we fall now, it causes us to grow in our hatred for sin as we see the ways it taints our relationship with God. Falling into sin causes us to passionately long to be with the Lord where we will be without sin. We cling more deeply to Jesus, are filled with more love for our Saviour and long more strongly to be with Him where He is. As we trip and stumble along the way, it causes us to cry out, *'Come, Lord Jesus!'*

 MEMORY VERSE
'Now to him who is able to keep you from stumbling and to present you blameless before the presence of his glory with great joy, to the only God, our Savior, through Jesus Christ our Lord, be glory, majesty, dominion, and authority, before all time and now and forever. Amen.' **Jude 24-25**

 SUMMARY
Every Christian is going to continue struggling with sin until we are glorified with Christ. The gospel promises us this reality, and empowers us along the journey as God keeps us and helps us even when we fall into sin.

God doesn't just want to leave us in our sins and work it all out in heaven. He wants us to confess our sins now as we live on this earth. How do we do that?

WHAT'S THE POINT?

PART OF OUR WAR AGAINST OUR SIN IS CONFESSING OUR SINS.

CONFESSING
OUR SINS

JOE

Joe has been struggling with various sins since he came to faith. Some-times it is lying, sometimes it is messing with drugs, other times it is lust. But he's not quite sure how and what he should be praying in these times. He feels like a fraud most of the time. He sins. He says sorry. He sins again. At his friend's church they go to the priest and the priest pronounces a blessing on them. That seems a bit easier than what Joe is doing. Sometimes, he's so ashamed he can't even pray and it is easier to lie than to admit what a scumbag he has been.

Again, we have to keep on repeating that **there is no such thing as perfect Christians this side of heaven**. Despite our best efforts and attempts to live godly lives, we still fail. We still sin. Christians try as hard as they can to *not* sin, and yet we still do. While we do seek to sin less now, our hope is not that we are sinless now but that **we are entirely forgiven now**. When Jesus saved us from our sins, he did so once for all. Through Christ, God has fully and entirely delivered us from the wages of our sin.

3X *'He has delivered us from the domain of darkness and transferred us to the kingdom of his beloved Son, in whom we have redemption, the forgiveness of sins.'* **Col. 1:13-14**

JOE

But if our sins — past, present and future — are fully forgiven then what does it matter if we sin? What do we do if we sin if you're saying Jesus has already forgiven them?

Good questions. <u>Joe needs to learn about the need for, and benefits of, confessing his sins</u>.

ILLUSTRATION

Imagine an Olympic runner who shows up to the 100m race wearing weights around his ankles. Now, in case you are not familiar with a 100m race, the goal is to run as fast as you possibly can in order to win the race. For this reason, runners usually wear tight and light clothing to run the most freely, that way their clothes would not get caught in the wind and slow them down. It would be foolish to wear weights on top of clothing that is designed for you to run most freely. No, before they would run well they must remove whatever additional weight there was so that they could run the most freely and strongly.

This is similar to how the Christian conscience works with shame from present sin. **It weighs the Christian down from living in the freedom of the gospel.** When we confess our sins, <u>the burden of sin is removed</u> as we are reminded through experience that our sins are truly and graciously forgiven.

We can know that we are forgiven as Christians because Jesus has promised this to us and we can count on His word. We also know that we are forgiven and belong to God because now when we do sin the Holy Spirit fills us with a sense of regret and shame. A person who is not truly a Christian will feel no shame in their sin. On the other hand, **Philippians 3:19** tells us that the sign of a non-believer is they *'glory in their shame.'* Christians, on the other hand, are weighed down by their shame. It's only through confession of their sins that Christians are able to take off all the weight of shame that would hinder their joy in Jesus and their running hard in the service of the Lord. ... Being weighed down with shame doesn't make anyone fruitful in the knowledge of the Lord.

It's true that we once happily lived in our sin. It was our most natural state.

'For we ourselves were once foolish, disobedient, led astray, slaves to various passions and pleasures, passing our days in malice and envy, hated by others and hating one another.' **Titus 3:3**

'...we all once lived in the passions of our flesh, carrying out the desires of the body and the mind, and were by nature children of wrath, like the rest of mankind.' **Ephesians 2:3**

STOP

Q: *What do these verses tell us about our attitude to sin before we became Christians?*

These verses remind us that <u>we loved our sin before Jesus saved us</u>.

We cherished our sin.
We revelled in it.
Every single day of our lives was given over to sinful living.

So, what's different now?

We don't live in sin.
We no longer live in the passions of the flesh.
We no longer carry out the desires of the body and the mind.
We fight against the passions of the world.
We fight against the spiritual attacks of the devil.
We fight to resist temptation.

The biggest way that we show all this to be true is that **we regularly confess our sins**.

Here comes the problem. Joe *instinctively* sees confession as a negative thing. Confessing sin sounds a lot like *becoming an informant*. In his mind you would be foolish to voluntarily offer up information to a crime you have already gotten away with. But <u>confession of sin is a biblical necessity in the life of a Christian</u>. Confession is:

Owning up — freely — to the fact that we have broken God's law.

Confession isn't merely admitting to a crime.
   Confession isn't having your arm twisted before owning up.

Confessing has often been explained to mean: **to say the same as**. In other words,

Confession suggests that you are admitting your full agreement.
   Confession is acknowledging that you share full agreement about
      something.

3X *'...if you confess with your mouth that Jesus is Lord and believe in your heart that God raised him from the dead, you will be saved.'* **Romans 10:9**

Note that the confession here is that **Jesus is Lord**. Now your confession doesn't make Jesus Lord (this is very important). Jesus is Lord anyway! So, all our confession is doing here is agreeing with the **FACT** that God's Word declares Jesus to be Lord.

In effect, *we are communicating that He is telling the truth about Jesus and we agree with Him.*

The same holds true when we confess our sins too. We are acknowledging that we agree with God about what sin really is. **Confession of our sins** isn't only a way to get rid of guilt (though it certainly is that), it **is first and foremost a humble acknowledgement of God's truthfulness**. We are acknowledging that, despite our actions, we truly believe what God says about sin and desire to evidence that through drawing attention to the ways we have contradicted His Word. This is what confession of sins does. It is proof that God's people now deal differently with their sin. Joe, and all Christians, are to be oriented differently towards sin than they previously were before they followed Jesus. No longer is sin simply something that we enjoy, it is a great evil that must be repented of. The Christian makes this clear when we faithfully and regularly confess our sins.

Nobody likes humiliation. Most people don't readily volunteer shameful information about themselves because of the cost it will have to their reputation. Shame lowers the honour we have in others' eyes as they see our true foolishness. But <u>the Christian works entirely differently</u>. We are called not to care what people think of us, but to rightly acknowledge what God has said concerning us. **We are called to go and inform on ourselves!**

ILLUSTRATION

Mirrors don't lie. No matter how good you think you look, or how well dressed you think you are — the mirror provides an unbiased perspective. Mirrors aren't given to flattery so they don't improve how you look in your reflection. What you see is simply what you are. If your reflection revealed to you that you had a huge hole in your shirt or dirt on your face, you would address the matter at once. You don't doubt the accuracy of your reflection because mirrors simply cannot lie.

Well, <u>God's Word is</u> referred to as <u>a mirror</u> in **James 1:23**. It doesn't lie but tells us who we really are. Therefore, <u>it is the things the Word of God calls sin that Christians are to regard as sin</u>. And in confession of our sins, we are agreeing with the Word's reflection, we are agreeing that **the rule of Christ is good** and that **we** need to be corrected **not** God. In confession of sins we are agreeing and acknowledging that we have lied with our actions about what is good while saying that God was right and true; We agree that we have lied and He cannot.

<u>We know that God knows everything about us</u>.

> **Jeremiah 17:10** teaches us that He searches the heart and tests the mind.
> **Jeremiah 17:9** teaches us that He knows that our hearts are deceitful and desperately sick.
> **Romans 2:16** teaches us that He will even judge the secrets of men.

God knows when we sin, and He is kind to afflict our conscience — to cause us to feel guilt and sorrow when we are sinning against Him so that we might confess our sins to Him and seek forgiveness. Hear these words from David, a servant of the Lord.

3X *'For when I kept silent, my bones wasted away through my groaning all day long. For day and night your hand was heavy upon me; my strength was dried up as by the heat of summer. I acknowledged my sin to you, and I did not cover my iniquity; I said, "I will confess my transgressions to the Lord," and you forgave the iniquity of my sin.'* **Psalm 32:3-5**

God dries up the joy of His children who are choosing sin rather than obedience to help them to understand the foolishness of their sin and to encourage them to confess their sins and be restored. All Christians still struggle against sin and, therefore, we should not be surprised to learn that **God calls all Christians to confess their sin**, too.

So, we've established that confession of sins is a good and a right thing to do. But who exactly do we confess our sins to?

(1) Confessing Our Sins to God.

Firstly, and <u>most importantly</u>, we always confess our sins to God before we do anything else.

3X *'If we confess our sins, he is faithful and just to forgive us our sins and to cleanse us from all unrighteousness.'* **1 John 1:9**

> **STOP**
> Q: Name the promises that God makes in this verse to those of us who are quick to confess our sins to him?

What a promise in this verse! <u>It is in confessing our sins to God that our consciences are washed clean.</u> When we sin, we make it hard to feel the forgiven state that we are in as God's children. We complicate our experience of God's love because we have chosen to take up the experience of sin. We feel <u>shame and guilt</u>, and <u>relational tension</u> with the Lord. He has saved us to serve Him in holiness, yet we are using our freedoms to disobey Him in sin. This <u>hurts</u> and <u>wounds</u> our consciences. But

through confession,
> we can draw near to God
>> and acknowledge our sin.

We can expose the darkness and it becomes light. In agreeing with God about our sin, <u>God washes us constantly in His forgiveness</u>. He reminds us through washing us of what Jesus died to secure — namely, the forgiveness of our sins.

And we have an incentive to come to the Lord and confess our sins. <u>He is faithful and just to forgive us and to cleanse us from all unrighteousness</u>. We don't confess our sins unsure of what God will do in return. God commands us to confess our sins so that we will be forgiven and cleansed! He is faithful to deal with us, consistent with His promise to be merciful to our iniquities and to remember our sins no more. Here's a great truth. When we confess our sins,

> **God WILL forgive us! He does what He says He will do.**

Why?

> **Because God cannot lie.**
> **He cannot and will not go against His own Word.**

<u>And His own Word promises us complete forgiveness when we come to him in confession of sin</u>.

This is why **God is just**. Because it would be unjust for God not to forgive us because Jesus has already paid for our forgiveness!

3X *'...But as it is, he has appeared once for all at the end of the ages to put away sin by the sacrifice of himself.'* **Hebrews 9:26**

Jesus has sacrificed Himself so that our sin would be <u>put away forever</u>, and God is just to deal with us according to the pardon Jesus bought for us!

See, Joe doesn't have to wallow in his shame and guilt whenever he sins.

He can come to God,
  confess his sin
    and experience the forgiveness and cleansing Jesus died to
      secure for him.

When we confess our sins we have no fear of judgment. God has promised us forgiveness forever, and He will be faithful and just to be consistent with that declaration.

(2) Confessing our Sins to Each Other.

The second part of confession is perhaps even more difficult than the first. We are far happier keeping our sins between ourselves and God. But the Bible encourages something altogether different.

3✕ *'...confess your sins to one another and pray for one another, that you may be healed.'* **James 5:16**

Apparently, not only would God zap the joy of His people who were practising sin, but He would even sometimes afflict them physically. But notice in this verse, we are encouraged to confess our sins not to further punishment, but **to be restored to health**. This doesn't mean that every time we have physical ailments it is because of sin. In **John 9:2-3**, Jesus' disciples thought a man was born blind because of someone's sin and Jesus abruptly corrects them: *'And his disciples asked him, "Rabbi, who sinned, this man or his parents, that he was born blind?" Jesus answered, "It was not that this man sinned, or his parents, but that the works of God might be displayed in him".'*

Not only are our physical ailments not always directly related to our sin, neither does prayer and confession always bring healing. Paul, says in **2 Corinthians 12:7-8** that he was hindered in his body, that the *'thorn was given me in the flesh, a messenger of Satan to harass me, to keep me from becoming conceited. Three times I pleaded with the Lord about this,* *that it should leave me.'* So, even he wasn't able to pray about his own healing!

The question remains then: **what is the benefit of confessing my sins to another Christian?**

Well, more important than our physical frame, <u>our soul is afflicted by sin</u>. Sin stains the soul and wounds our heart's ability to relate to God. David, in **Psalm 51:8**, describes the fracture in his relationship with the Lord, caused by his own sin, as like his bones being broken. As we confess our sins to one another we are admitting before God our need for help and <u>asking a brother or sister in Christ to bear our burdens with us</u>. They, like any friend helping the wounded along, bear us up on their shoulders in prayer and walk with us to the throne of grace to obtain mercy and help that heals.

MEMORY VERSE

'If we confess our sins, he is faithful and just to forgive us our sins and to cleanse us from all unrighteousness.' **1 John 1:9**

SUMMARY

Christians aren't perfect. In fact, we are far from it. One primary way that Christians display this is through confessing our sins, both to God and to one another. In confession we are agreeing with God's view about sin and our need for forgiveness from Him. Thankfully, God is faithful and just to forgive us and cleanse us from every sin based on the gospel of Jesus Christ.

WHAT'S THE POINT?

SOONER OR LATER THINGS WILL BECOME VERY DIFFICULT BUT WE MUST PERSEVERE.

HITTING THE WALL (PERSEVERANCE)

RECAP

When we are saved by Jesus we enter a lifelong spiritual war.
The whole world is hostile to the things of God.
We have a powerful spiritual enemy who is out to destroy us.
We are called to fight and guaranteed to win.
We need a plan to fight against our spiritual enemies in this world.
This side of glory, failing will be a normal part of every Christian's life.
Part of our war against our sin is confessing our sins.

JOE

Joe is finding the going really tough. The buzz and excitement he had in the early months of becoming a Christian is wearing off. Christianity has lost its 'newness' and the shine is starting to wear off. He feels like he has run into a brick wall and he is tempted to go back to his old way of life. That seems easier than trying to live for Jesus. Anything seems easier than trying to live an obedient Christian life. Why is it that all the other Christians in church seem to breeze through their lives but he feels like he is walking through quicksand? He wants to give up.

STOP

Q: *What is your advice to Joe? Is he the only person who feels like this in the Christian life? What should he do?*

ILLUSTRATION

Marathon and long distance runners often use an expression called, '**hitting the wall.**' It usually happens several miles into a run when all their energy suddenly goes and every step they run is excruciatingly difficult. They feel like it is almost impossible to go on. They feel general weakness, fatigue, dizziness and some even report hallucinations. It is at this point that mental toughness plays a part. Some runners continue through the barrier and others just give in. Everybody experiences the wall at some point and everybody handles it differently.

Joe needs to know that every single Christian will 'hit the wall' at some point in their Christian experience. In fact, the Christian life is something of an obstacle course. Just when we think we have one part of it beaten, up pops another in our way. In order to survive the wall, and all the other obstacles that will come our way, we must **persevere**. Another great word that means the same thing is, **steadfastness**. What do these words mean?

ILLUSTRATION

Have you ever seen weightlifters at the Olympic Games? Sometimes they lift incredible weights, far more than their own body weight. One of the keys to a successful power lift is the positon of the legs. It is noticeable how much time the athlete spends getting their body position and legs right before they attempt to lift the weight. They plant their feet firmly on the ground and they lean into the weight steadfastly before they attempt their lift.

In **James 1:3** we read that trials produce this kind of perseverance or steadfastness in us. In other words, when we hit the wall or when <u>trials come we should stand super firm. James is basically saying that trials prove that what we believe is genuine</u>. **When trials come the true Christian is not destroyed and their faith remains firm**. Trials show where our allegiances truly lie. That's why two people from the same church can be diagnosed with Cancer and one can become shrivelled and bitter against God and the other can draw near to him and persevere in faith. That moment of testing has proved the genuineness of the faith they professed.

<u>God wants to develop our characters and produce a spirit of perseverance in us</u> and the best way for that to happen is through trials. Trials help the true Christian to hold on to Jesus. To keep going. To keep standing. So many people today can't handle pressure. They are immature. They have never

taken on trials. They have run from them or tried to medicate their way out of them.

Perseverance means:

> *We keep going in the face of:*
> > **pain**
> > **disappointment**
> > **discomfort.**
> *We don't quit:*
> > **when trials come.**
> *We remain faithful:*
> > **when life is going against us.**
> *We stick it out:*
> > **until the end.**

3X *'In this world you will have trouble.'* **John 16:33** (NIV)

'We must go through many hardships to enter the kingdom of God' **Acts 14:22** (NIV)

'Dear friends, do not be surprised at the painful trial you are suffering, as though something strange were happening to you' **1 Peter 4:12** (NIV)

> **STOP**
> Q: *What are these verses telling us about what we Christians should expect in this life?*

Just listen to how the great Apostle Paul suffered in his life, despite his faithfulness to the Lord Jesus.

3X *'As servants of God we commend ourselves in every way: in great endurance; in troubles, hardships and distresses; in beatings, imprisonments and riots; in hard work, sleepless nights and hunger; in purity, understanding, patience and kindness; in the Holy Spirit and in sincere love; in truthful* *speech and in the power of God; with weapons of righteousness in the right hand and in the left; through glory and dishonour, bad report and good report; genuine, yet regarded as impostors; known, yet regarded as unknown; dying, and yet we live on; beaten, and yet not killed; sorrowful, yet always rejoicing; poor, yet making many rich; having nothing, and yet possessing everything.* **2 Corinthians 6:4–10** (NIV)

This was a bloke who knew what it was like to hit the wall! Many times! Yet we read in **2 Timothy 3:10-11** that he *'endured'* them all. Joe has to wake up to the reality that <u>struggle will now be a part of his life until God calls him home</u>. We live in an imperfect world and we get to watch our loved ones:

> **Get old.**
> **Get sick.**
> **Die.**

These are the facts of life. <u>There is nothing we can do to avoid them</u>. We can't go to the gym enough. We can't eat enough healthy food. We can't get drunk enough. We can't get high enough. We can't get enough sex. We can't make enough money. We can't watch enough television. <u>Most people think Christians don't live in the real world</u>. It's just **not true**. The Bible is nothing if not realistic. It prepares us for the real world. It makes us face up to the reality of our existence here on earth. <u>We are merely people who are just passing through</u>.

Now, some of our trials are self-inflicted.

> **We smoke forty cigarettes a day and then get Cancer.**
> **We drink too much and get liver disease.**
> **We max out our credit cards and get swamped in debt.**
> **We get involved in a sinful relationship and it collapses.**

<u>We cannot blame the Lord for things we do to ourselves</u>.

But, there are trials outside of our control.

We are diagnosed with a degenerative illness.
Somebody crashed into our car.
Our house is set on fire by faulty wiring.

The problem with life is that trials come upon us and they often catch us completely unaware. Life is going fine and then boom – disaster strikes! Sometimes, if we're really honest, <u>we just get tired of the endless discipline of walking in holiness</u>. It even gets boring!

JOE

So, you're saying that this is normal? That everybody hits the wall? Those trials affect everybody? SO, what am I supposed to do about it then? What's the point? Why does God let this stuff happen? Why doesn't He sort it out for me?

STOP

Q: What do you think? How would you answer Joe's questions?

 '...because you know that the testing of your faith produces perseverance. Let perseverance finish its work so that you may be mature and complete, not lacking anything.' **James 1:3-4** (NIV)

Joe needs to understand that <u>perseverance has a job to do in his life</u>. What job?

God wants to perfect us so that we lack for nothing. That's what he tells us in v. 4. The way He makes us perfect is as <u>we persevere through trials</u>. Each time we come through a trial with our faith intact and our hearts still warm toward Jesus we are actually growing in perfection and completeness. We are becoming Christ-like. So what feels like punishment to Joe is in some way completing him as a human being.

<u>Far too many Christians are so used to the lie that says God only does good stuff in us when He does good stuff for us.</u>

<u>But most of the good stuff in terms of building us up in our faith is done in the bad stuff of life</u>.

Think about it: many of us lack real empathy with people until we have suffered ourselves. Many of us lack patience with young mothers whose children fuss in the service and cry out and yet we view it differently when we have been through the experience ourselves. We have more patience. We pray for those of our number who are sick but it is only when we become really sick ourselves that we really understand their pain.

Suffering helps us to grow and mature as believers.
Suffering helps us to love and care for one another better.
Suffering helps us to lean on Jesus.

So trials come. They are a fact of life. The wall hits us. It is a common Christian experience. God wants to use these things so that we persevere in the faith and also to help us grow into maturity. So, how should we pray in the light of all of this information? After all, how many prayers do we hear in church that say something along these lines:

Lord, cure my friend's sickness.
Lord, I hope we have a good holiday.
Lord, I hope I get that job.
Lord, take this trial from me.

But is this what God wants? Is this how He wants Joe, and us, to pray in the midst of our difficulties? The answer is actually quite surprising.

 'If any of you lacks wisdom, you should ask God, who gives generously to all without finding fault, and it will be given to you.' **James 1:5** (NIV)

What's unusual about this verse is that normally we would expect people to pray for a healing, or for deliverance or for God to take away whatever is causing the suffering. But instead James connects persevering under trial <u>to praying for wisdom</u>. (I want to talk about it a little bit in this chapter but we are going to look at this topic in more detail in our next book in the series).

Wisdom is asking God to help us know what is right and true in a given situation.

Wisdom is what Job cries out for in the middle of his terrible distress in **Job 28:12, 23, 28**. *But where can wisdom be found? Where does understanding dwell? God understands the way to it and he alone knows where it dwells, And He said to the human race, 'The fear of the Lord — that is wisdom, and to shun evil is understanding'.* (NIV)

Wisdom just seems like a weird thing to ask for when we are suffering. Normally, when we are in trouble our prayers sound something like this.

Help me Lord.
Take this from me Lord.
Get me out of this situation Lord.
I promise never to do it again if you just sort this out for me one more time.

Many of us think of asking for God's wisdom when it comes to changing jobs or moving house or making a big decision. But here James is using it when talking about trials. What advice do we get from unbelieving family and friends when struggles come? What advice do they have? What is their wisdom in the face of extreme suffering? They get angry. They maybe say they hate God. But what wisdom do they give? What godly, helpful insight do they give into a given situation? We cannot get our wisdom from the world. In times of trouble we have to run to God for wisdom.

3X *'But the wisdom that comes from heaven is first of all pure; then peace-loving, considerate, submissive, full of mercy and good fruit, impartial and sincere.'* **James 3:17** (NIV)

'The Lord gives wisdom, from His mouth comes knowledge and understanding. He stores up sound wisdom for the upright.' **Proverbs 2:6**

'The fear of the Lord is the beginning of wisdom, and knowledge of the Holy One is understanding.' **Proverbs 9:10** (NIV)

'Eat honey, my son, for it is good; honey from the comb is sweet to your taste. Know also that wisdom is like honey for you: If you find it, there is a future hope for you, and your hope will not be cut off.' **Proverbs 24:13-14** (NIV)

STOP

Q: *What do we learn about wisdom from these verses?*

We need to run to God in our darkest moments. We need to run to God and ask him for wisdom to be able to see through the fog and work out what He is trying to teach us through our difficulties.

JOE

Is that it? Ask for wisdom? That all sounds a bit too easy. There must be more to it than that?

There is.

 'But when you ask, you must believe and not doubt, because the one who doubts is like a wave of the sea, blown and tossed by the wind.' **James 1:6** (NIV)

The key to asking for wisdom from God is found in v. 6. **We must do it without doubting.** We must do it trusting by faith that God hears us. We have no need to doubt God's goodness in our lives. Yet we all worry when we come up against a particular difficulty in life.

Worry is just doubting that God will keep His Word.

Some of us may ask for God's wisdom but we don't really want it. Really, we want Him to act according to our wisdom. We come to Him like Father Christmas with our list and get in a strop when we get something completely different. But we need to trust that God has got everything under control for our lives.

We may not see it.

We may not even agree with it.

But God has it all under control.

Those who doubt these truths are described as people blown around and tossed about by the wind. In other words, unstable. People who get jumpy at the first sign of difficulty.

Maybe God is not answering prayer as quickly as we'd like.

Maybe we have gotten ourselves into a sticky situation and God hasn't come immediately to our rescue.

Maybe we are full of doubt and fear about whether our faith is genuine.

Many of us don't receive God's wisdom because we are racked with worry, bitterness, envy, fear and doubt. Up and down: unstable. Do we wonder why the church is full of people who have prayed about certain things and are left disillusioned because they didn't get the answer they wanted? We treat God like a little vending machine. Say a prayer and pick the answer you want. Don't get it. Then there's something wrong with the machine. So many of us make awful decisions saying I've prayed about it but what they mean is that they maybe prayed once or twice but not very much and with little real faith. People who don't read the Bible very much, don't have a regular worship time with the Lord, don't really associate with His people in the church and then when trouble comes thinks a few short prayers will make it all right. That is not Christianity. That is witchcraft. You might as well go and get yourself a rabbit's foot. Useless. Don't bother. God will not answer those kinds of attitudes to prayer.

If we want His wisdom, to make good decisions when our emotions are all over the place, then we need to do it without doubting. We need to rest in His grace and truth and love.

3X **1 Peter 4:12**, *'Beloved, do not be surprised at the fiery ordeal among you, which comes upon you for your testing, as though some strange thing were happening to you; ...'* (NASB)

> **STOP**
>
> Q: How does this verse help us help someone like Joe, somebody who has hit the wall in their Christian faith?

So, a Christian receives bad news. **It's Cancer**. Of course there is the initial shock.

> Then fear.
> > Then anger.
> > > Then maybe helplessness.

But when we start to consider it as Christians, **we realise that we have a hope**. We have Christ. **We can have a peace**. We can think past the problem and see the bigger picture. The world can't. It lives for now. A diagnosis like that is death for the unbeliever. For the Christian we see a bigger picture.

> Maybe we didn't get the job we wanted.
> Maybe a situation hasn't worked out how we wanted it to.
> Maybe a relationship didn't go as planned.
> Maybe I'm not where I thought I would be when I was in my 20s.

Never let anybody tell you that Satan is sending you trials. Satan does nothing without God's permission. **God is allowing trials in our lives for a greater purpose and we have to rejoice in the situation even when logic screams otherwise**. He's not saying be happy you're suffering. He's saying be joyful for what the trial is going to accomplish in you. But God can use all of them to grow us and perfect us. They can be used for our good. **Even hitting the wall can be a chance for real spiritual development**. How can Joe do more than hang on and live joyfully in the middle of his trials? Because HE KNOWS all of these things.

 MEMORY VERSE

'...being confident of this, that he who began a good work in you will carry it on to completion until the day of Christ Jesus.' **Philippians 1:6** (NIV)

📍 **SUMMARY**

The Christian life is not easy. We are at war. This battle is about who you worship – God or Satan. Everything seems to be against us. Each new day the world, our flesh and Satan fight against us, seeking to distract us and deceive us into denying Christ. It is intense! Yet we also know that we are guaranteed to win. So let's not act like we are defeated, saying the struggle is too hard for us to bear, rather let's get in the fight.

Every Christian will *'hit the wall'* in their Christian life. Every Christian will face trials of many kinds throughout their life. It is nothing unusual. The Christian, therefore, has to learn to persevere as they trust in God's work for their life. God will use these times to mould our character and make us more like Jesus. These things will help us grow to maturity and we must ask the Lord for wisdom to stick close. Ask without fear and without doubt and you will stand firm to the end.

JOE

For Joe, the battles are just beginning. When he first accepted Jesus as his saviour he was full of excitement that he is forgiven and accepted. It was a great moment. He wasn't prepared for how hard things would become. With his friends, his kids, even the battles that go on in his own head – there are times he feels so weak. There are so many voices screaming at him – some of the loudest are the ones telling him just to give up on Jesus. Other voices are telling him he is not good enough, he won't ever be good enough, just give up and stop trying to be someone he isn't. One thing Joe has come to know is that he can't do this alone. He needs other Christians to help him, to guide him and keep him encouraged.

Stick with it Joe. There are other battles coming...

IX 9Marks

Building Healthy Churches

9Marks exists to equip church leaders with a biblical vision and practical resources for displaying God's glory to the nations through healthy churches.

To that end, we want to see churches characterized by these nine marks of health:

1   Expositional Preaching
2   Biblical Theology
3   A Biblical Understanding of the Gospel
4   A Biblical Understanding of Conversion
5   A Biblical Understanding of Evangelism
6   Biblical Church Membership
7   Biblical Church Discipline
8   Biblical Discipleship
9   Biblical Church Leadership

Find more titles at
www.9Marks.org

20schemes

Gospel Churches for Scotland's Poorest

20schemes exists to bring gospel hope to Scotland's poorest communities through the revitalization and planting of healthy, gospel-preaching churches, ultimately led by a future generation of indigenous church leaders.

> *"If we are really going to see a turnaround in the lives of residents in our poorest communities, then we have to embrace a radical and long-term strategy which will bring gospel-hope to untold thousands."*
>
> **MEZ MCCONNELL,** Ministry Director

We believe that building healthy churches in Scotland's poorest communities will bring true, sustainable, and long-term renewal to countless lives.

THE NEED IS URGENT

Learn more about our work and how to partner with us at:

20SCHEMES.COM
TWITTER.COM/20SCHEMES
FACEBOOK.COM/20SCHEMES
INSTAGRAM.COM/20SCHEMES

Christian Focus Publications

Our mission statement –

STAYING FAITHFUL

In dependence upon God we seek to impact the world through literature faithful to His infallible Word, the Bible. Our aim is to ensure that the Lord Jesus Christ is presented as the only hope to obtain forgiveness of sin, live a useful life and look forward to heaven with Him.

Our Books are published in four imprints:

CHRISTIAN
FOCUS

popular works including biographies, commentaries, basic doctrine and Christian living.

CHRISTIAN
HERITAGE

books representing some of the best material from the rich heritage of the church.

MENTOR

books written at a level suitable for Bible College and seminary students, pastors, and other serious readers. The imprint includes commentaries, doctrinal studies, examination of current issues and church history.

CF4•K

children's books for quality Bible teaching and for all age groups: Sunday school curriculum, puzzle and activity books; personal and family devotional titles, biographies and inspirational stories – because you are never too young to know Jesus!

Christian Focus Publications Ltd,
Geanies House, Fearn, Ross-shire,
IV20 1TW, Scotland, United Kingdom.
www.christianfocus.com